W9-AJQ-632

BEYOND THE THRONE

THE ENDURING LEGACY OF EMPEROR HAILE SELASSIE I

BY INDRIAS GETACHEW

EDITED BY RICHARD PANKHURST

FOREWORD BY HAROLD MARCUS

SHAMA BOOKS

ADDIS ABABA, ETHIOPIA

2001

A division of TRANCO P.L.C.
Addis Ababa, Ethiopia

First edition 2001

PUBLISHED BY
Shama Books
P.O. Box 8153
Addis Ababa
Ethiopia

Distribution in partnership with New Line Press, USA

ISBN 1-931253-00-5
ISBN 1-931253-03-X BOX SET

DESIGNED BY
John and Orna Designs, London

All images courtesy of the Institute of Ethiopian Studies,
Addis Ababa University

CONTENTS

ACKNOWLEDGEMENTS

To my mother and father who raised me, and sacrificed so much to educate me, thank you. To all my siblings and family whose love and support has been unconditional and unwavering, blessings. Yasser Bagersh and Jonathan Niehaus at Shama Books, much respect – your patience, goodwill, and the tremendous effort you put in to see this magnificent project through to completion is much appreciated – thank you for choosing to work with me. To the numerous friends and supporters who granted interviews and allowed me the privilege of using their libraries to research the subject, much gratitude. Thank you Dr. Richard Pankhurst for reading my manuscript, for your comments and suggestions, as well as for correcting my historical errors; and my thanks to Professor Harold Marcus for writing the foreword to this book.

Above all, many thanks and praises 'le Ityopia Amlak', the God of Ethiopia for granting me this unparalleled heritage, and the chance to share my perspective on Ethiopia. I am humbled by the story that I have tried to relate. It feels mighty good to be Ethiopian and my prayers are for good fortune to finally break through and rain down on this ancient land and civilization so that we may at last once more stand dignified and proud among the family of nations.

INDRIAS GETACHEW

FOREWORD

IN CONTEMPORARY ETHIOPIA, THERE ARE NO SQUARES, HOSPITALS, SCHOOLS, BOULEVARDS, AND THE LIKE THAT BEAR THE NAME OF EMPEROR HAILE SELASSIE I (1892-1975). HAD HE DIED BEFORE THE REVOLUTION OF 1974, HIS NAME AND ACHIEVEMENTS WOULD TODAY BE CELEBRATED. INSTEAD, HE WAS DEPOSED BY A MILITARY CLIQUE THAT VILIFIED HIM AS THE CAUSE OF ETHIOPIA'S MANY ILLS AND THEN TRANSFORMED HIM INTO AN UNPERSON. THE NEW GOVERNMENT'S PROPAGANDA APPARATUS EITHER TOTALLY IGNORED HAILE SELASSIE'S REIGN OR RECALLED HIM AS A SCAPEGOAT FOR ITS OWN FAULTS AND FAILURES.

Although the emperor lived on in the minds of older Ethiopians, he was lost to the younger generation who learned their history from books that rendered events and personalities from a highly politicized point of view. It is little wonder that those thirty or younger, now the majority of people in Ethiopia, know little about Haile Selassie. Indrias Getachew's book seeks to restore the emperor to his proper place in history and to relate his story to a generation of Ethiopians ignorant of the facts of his reign. The pictures in this book, many of them previously unpublished, try and show the emperor in both personal and official settings.

Except for the period of the Italian war and occupation, 1934-1941, the emperor presided over a time of growth, development, optimism, and peace. As the architect of the modern state, he managed his country's entry into the world, in the process becoming a global figure. During the 1920s and 1930s, he busily modernized and centralized the government through the introduction of uniform administration and legal structures and the appointment of a newly educated elite to positions of authority in Addis Ababa and in the provinces; and reformed and re-equipped the Ethiopian army and police by providing up-to-date training and weaponry. Since the costs of the new age were high, H.I.M. led Ethiopia toward

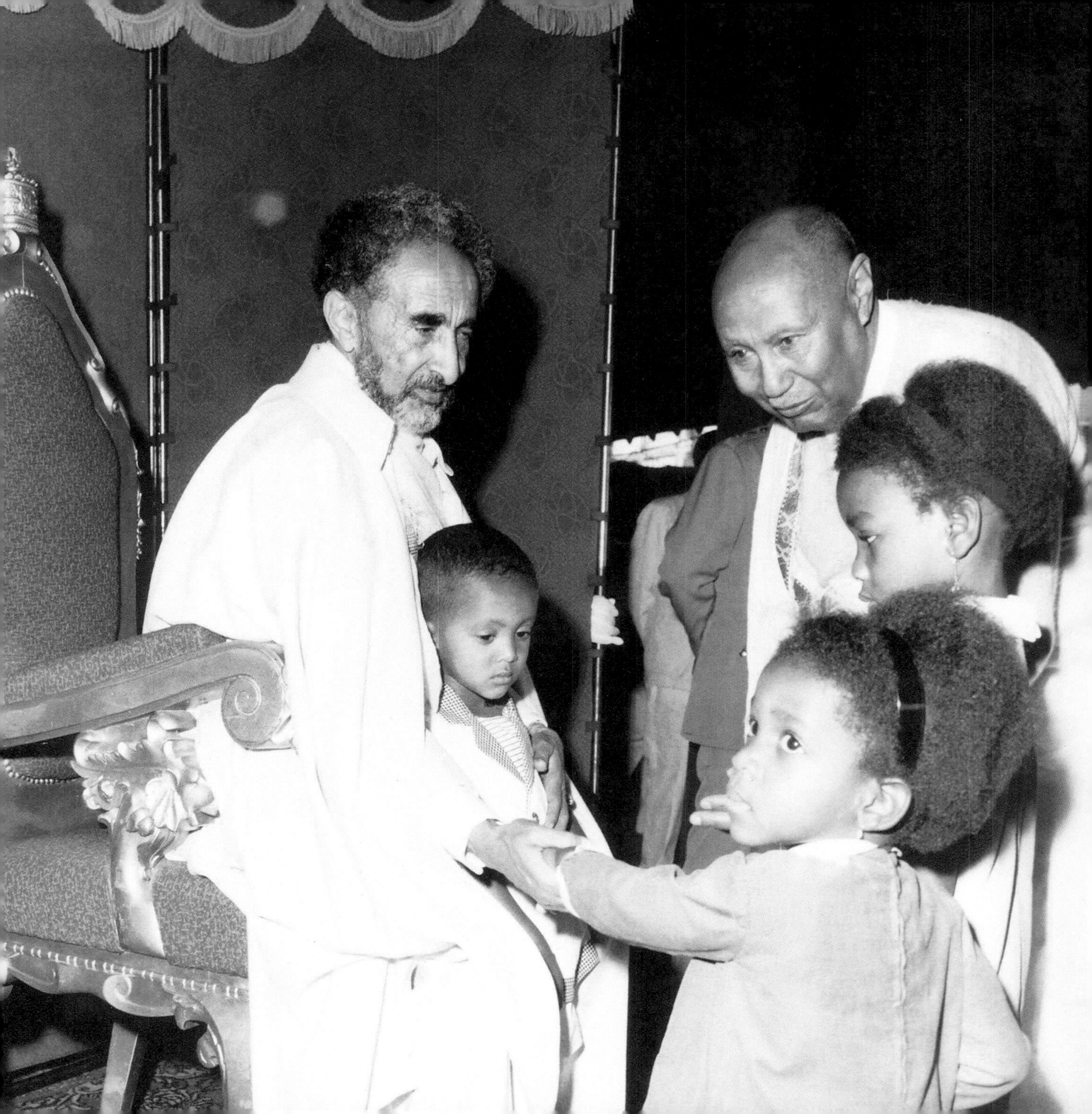

capitalistic agriculture in coffee, oil seeds, and cereal in demand in the Middle East. Working with the aristocracy, foreign merchants, indigenous traders, and the government bureaucracy, Haile Selassie created an export economy to provide revenues for development. Upon returning to Ethiopia in 1941, he immediately reverted to the pre-war economy to garner enough funds to continue his policies of modernization.

He built a standing army to provide internal security and to police the frontiers, a permanent bureaucracy to achieve uniform governance from Addis Ababa, modern communications to tie the country together, and a national economy to raise the standard of living of his subjects wherever they lived in the empire. He finished his historic task of redefining the authority and functions of the landed aristocracy to strengthen his increasingly centralized state. He introduced modern legal codes to ensure equal justice for all under the rule of law, new forms of taxation to standardize payments nationwide, parliamentary government through direct election of representatives, a national airline, and a modern system of education.

From the few thousand students of the pre-war state, the educational system grew to hundreds of thousands by 1974. H.I.M. was the architect of higher studies in Ethiopia and he had an almost religious belief in the modernizing effect of western education on the nation's youth. For many years, he was titular Minister of Education and chairman of the intergovernmental Board of Education. He had a special place in his heart for students at all levels. He visited their schools, he sampled the food they ate, he gave them gifts of clothing and fruit, he questioned them about their studies, and he spoke to them about the importance of their education for the nation and for himself as their monarch. By doing so, he was not building a cult of personality but merely revealing the paternalism he felt toward his subjects, especially toward the young people who were Ethiopia's future.

Besides seeing himself as the father of the nation, Haile Selassie viewed himself as the embodiment of Ethiopia's proud sovereignty and independence. His national vision, a legacy from his father Ras Makonnen (1854-1906), who administered Harerge from Emperor Menelik (r. 1889-1913), comprised an elite that governed a polyglot, often non-Christian, population. The latter could assimilate into the power structure by acculturating to the Amhara – if not Christian – culture of the rulers. At first, many Ethiopians regarded this transition as normal, if annoying, but as the 20th century became the age of ethnicity and minority rights, assimilation in Ethiopia became personally, then politically, insulting. No amount of imperial paternalism could redress the cultural hurt felt by Ethiopia's nationalities, and H.I.M. was unable to change his monomania about Amharic 'as the Mother of the Nation.'

He continued to govern, as had his predecessors, by acting as the country's balancer of power, a method that worked well in a customary government that mediated between the ruling classes and the masses. Modern administration, however, required institutions that permitted the development of competing political ideas and the transfer of power from one set of elites to another. The emperor's limited western education directed him toward change but only in terms of enhancing imperial power and adding to the central government that acted in his name. With no institutionalized outlet for their political goals and ambitions, the newly educated, in the 1960s and 1970s, agitated for any change that would free them from the political inertia of the emperor's no-party, paternalistic state. They adopted a simplistic and wrong-headed Marxist ideology and thereby mistook the decade's economic change and the creation of capital in the countryside as stemming from the ruling elite's crude exploitation of the peasantry.

By 1972, the emperor was a very old man who displayed signs of senility. He was exhausted by the new ideological politics and emotionally distressed by the apparent betrayal of the children whom he had educated and favored. His government was fighting rebels in Eritrea, Bale, and even Gojam over the question of ethnicity and political rights. The bureaucratic bourgeoisie wanted more authority in developing policy and administration. H.I.M.'s love affair with the United States appeared to be ending as Washington's strategic interests in the Red Sea were better served by Egypt and Israel, now American allies, and as the communications base in Asmara was rendered obsolete by satellites. Haile Selassie's vision of a peaceful, stable Ethiopia was contradicted by the realities surrounding him, and he never seemed to know his time was past, which is why he never took any of the several opportunities he had to smash the students and, as late as June 1974, even the Dergue. To the last, Haile Selassie remained a humane Christian and a true Ethiopian patriot, unwilling to spill his compatriot's blood even for the sake of his empire. We shall not see his like again, which is why Indrias Getachew has written this Ethiopian appreciation for the greatest Ethiopian ruler of all time.

BY HAROLD MARCUS, MICHIGAN STATE UNIVERSITY

1962–63 ADDIS ABABA

PORTRAIT OF THE ROYAL FAMILY

INTRODUCTION

TWENTY-FIVE YEARS AGO, ON AUGUST 27 1975 ETHIOPIA'S LAST EMPEROR, HIS IMPERIAL MAJESTY EMPEROR HAILE SELASSIE I, PASSED AWAY UNDER CIRCUMSTANCES THAT HAVE YET TO BE SATISFACTORILY EXPLAINED. HE HAD RULED ETHIOPIA FOR CLOSE TO SIXTY YEARS; FOURTEEN OF THOSE AS CROWN PRINCE AND REGENT, AND JUST UNDER FORTY-FOUR AS EMPEROR.

During this impressive career, Emperor Haile Selassie guided the ancient empire of Ethiopia into the modern era. Under him, an isolated Ethiopia successfully integrated into the larger family of nations during a century characterized by ever shrinking borders and increasingly interconnected human existence.

For at least 3000 years, Ethiopia was ruled by monarchs who reigned over a conservative and pious society described in Homer's *Iliad* as 'the blameless Ethiopians.' As though to preserve that generous characterization, historic and geographic influences conspired to keep the peoples of the Horn of Africa's highland massifs isolated from the rest of the world with only scarce contact over the millennia. In that isolated fastness developed a unique and little known civilization that in the 21st century still retains the trappings of an entirely different era.

During the twentieth century, the outside world became an important factor in the previously detached Ethiopian reality. Dramatic change characterized the twentieth century experience, and Emperor Haile Selassie bore the exclusive responsibility of charting a course into this radically new era. Within Ethiopia, he struggled to have his people embrace the positive offerings of the outside world, as well as to realize the dangers that continued isolation meant in a time of unprecedented military technological advancement. Outside

Ethiopia, he fought to elevate the position of Ethiopia among the family of nations, an uphill struggle fraught with all the hazards of racism and prejudice.

At the beginning of his political career, Emperor Haile Selassie stood alone among the Ethiopian nobility, with virtually none of the establishment sharing his dreams of a new and modern Ethiopia. His vision for Ethiopia put him at odds with his contemporaries, and it is a testament to his character and capability as a leader that he was able to succeed in bringing modernity to an archaic system.

Emperor Haile Selassie's contributions to the development of contemporary Ethiopia were monumental. Yet despite his indisputable record of effort and accomplishment, his final days were not only tragic but remain an embarrassment to all Ethiopians; twenty-five years after the death of Ethiopia's last emperor he has yet to receive a proper burial.

The Revolution of 1974 brought out the demons in Ethiopian society. People who for decades had prostrated themselves before the emperor now jeered and booed him as he was driven to prison in the back of a Volkswagen Beetle. The forces responsible for his downfall had completely lost sight of the fact that they owed their very existence to his endeavors to modernize Ethiopia. The students who attended school thanks to his untiring efforts to establish a modern school system; the military which owed its training and weapons to him; the urban workers who were the beneficiaries of his development efforts; all turned on him in the ugliest manner.

The remains of Emperor Haile Selassie were discovered in 1992, shortly after the fall of the Dergue regime. Eight years later, Ethiopia's last emperor has yet to be accorded the basic dignity of a decent funeral. Over the course of this last decade, a group of interested institutions and individuals, including members of the imperial family, formed the Haile Selassie I Memorial Foundation. This Foundation has now taken on the sole responsibility of arranging the funeral of the emperor. Several months ago, the Foundation announced that the long awaited event would take place during the year 2000. *(The latest information at the time of this writing is that it is planned for 5 November 2000)* As his burial approaches, we are presented with an opportunity to look back on the life and times of one of the greatest and most influential rulers in Ethiopian history and to bid farewell to a man that friend and foe alike will concur was a formidable statesman and leader.

The passing of time has allowed those Ethiopians who had the privilege of experiencing his reign to compare what we had with what has come after. When I hear my elders speak about that time, it is with bittersweet nostalgia, their voices heavy with regret and resignation for an era that has now passed. Though I was only three years old when the emperor passed away, I believe that those times were better in many respects. This is not to argue that there were no problems or that the calls for reform that precipitated the events of 1974 were unjustified. What is disturbing is the manner in which things were handled, for not only did we lose an integral part of what it meant to be Ethiopian – 3000 years of royalty and all the cultural attachments that come with it – we also lost our dignity. Ethiopia today faces a whole host of challenges and if we are to have any hope for the future, one of our immediate tasks will be to recapture that dignity and the moral character needed to prevail in meeting our current challenges.

The images included in this book, many of which are being published for the first time, are filled with those twin elements of dignity and character. They are reminders of a time in the not too distant past when the name Ethiopia was not associated solely with famine and war. Instead, 'Abyssinia' and 'Ethiopia' conjured images of a romantic struggle to wake up from what has been described as a 3000 year slumber. Not everyone who has come into contact with Ethiopia has been charmed. However, the experience invariably is one that will never be forgotten.

The enduring legacy of one of the longest reigning monarchs in recent world history has continued to grow stronger, forever evolving and manifesting itself in new and increasingly dynamic ways. Emperor Haile Selassie is not only immortalized as the last Ethiopian emperor, the sometimes unloved father of contemporary Ethiopians, he is also the spiritual father of modern day independent Africa.

Haile Selassie is even celebrated to the point of deification by some members of the African diaspora, namely the Rastafarians. Rastafarianism, so named after Haile Selassie's pre-coronation name and born of the back-to-Africa teachings of Marcus Garvey in the opening decades of the twentieth century, is based on a prophecy that a king would arise in Africa who would lead his people to liberty. That prophecy came true for believers when Emperor Haile Selassie I became the *Neguse Negest*, or King of Kings, of Ethiopia. As a man who would become a leader in the anti-colonial movement, and the ruler of the one African nation to maintain 3000 years of independence, Haile Selassie was the fulfillment of Marcus Garvey's prophecies. For Rastafarians, Emperor Haile Selassie is the reincarnation of the Holy Savior, and they remain his most ardent champions.

Haile Selassie's contributions have yet to be fully acknowledged and appreciated by the people he once led and the country he left behind. This book is an attempt to reflect on his life and on the last chapters in a story that spans three millennia. This text does not pretend to be an exhaustive account of Emperor Haile Selassie's life. It is rather an attempt to recapture the essence of his epic experience as the last Ethiopian emperor, to retell his story so that we may have a better understanding of our past, to pause and reflect on the foundations upon which we are attempting to build our future. It is also an invitation for non-Ethiopians to refresh their perspectives of this ancient land and peoples with the hope of removing the stigma that several decades of media reports that focus solely on famine and war have created.

NOTE:

All dates in this book are in accordance with the Gregorian Calendar, not the Julian Calendar which is used in Ethiopia. Some years are listed as two years (1973-74) to accommodate this conversion from the Julian to the Gregorian.

EXAMPLES OF TRADITIONAL ETHIOPIAN CROWNS AND CROSSES

HISTORICAL HERITAGE

ETHIOPIA, AN ANCIENT LAND POSSESSING A TREMENDOUS CULTURAL AND HISTORICAL LEGACY, IS ALSO ONE OF THE LONGEST POPULATED AREAS OF THE WORLD. THIS FACT IS TESTIFIED TO BY SEVERAL REMARKABLE DISCOVERIES INCLUDING THE MOST CELEBRATED SKELETAL FIND IN HISTORY; THE OVER THREE MILLION YEAR OLD 'LUCY', OR AS SHE IS CALLED BY HER MODERN DAY COMPATRIOTS 'DINKINESH', GENERALLY TRANSLATED AS 'THOU ART MARVELOUS/UNIQUE'. ETHIOPIA CAN CLAIM TO BE THE 'CRADLE OF MANKIND' – THE STARTING POINT OF THE HUMAN RACE AND THE BEGINNING OF ALL HUMAN HISTORY. THIS ETHIOPIAN ASSERTION IS PRODIGIOUS AND BOASTS OF AN UNPARALLELED PATRIMONY.

The Ethiopian story reaches back into the obscure and prehistoric past, as well as to the dawn of recorded human history. What is clear is that Ethiopia ranked among the major civilizations of what we generally refer to as the ancient world – the civilizations that flourished from two to three millennia ago. Through her extensive trading links to Asia, India, and the Mediterranean world, Ethiopia served as a major crossroads of civilizations, and as a bridge between Africa and the Middle East.

Historical references to Ethiopia go as far back as the third millennium B.C. with Pharaonic records of expeditions sent to Punt, the Land of the Gods, believed to be what is present day Ethiopia. Egyptian ships traded for incense, scented woods, slaves, ivory and other items in a land fabled for its wealth and fantastic resources.

The earliest evidence of settlement indicates significant migratory patterns in what are today northern Ethiopia and Eritrea. Archaeological findings from the Red Sea coast, as well as from a line of former settlements and towns going inland towards Axum, provide proof of a civilization similar to what existed in Southern Arabia. Temple ruins and artifacts uncovered at the ancient site of Yeha, approximately thirty kilometers outside of Axum, bear witness to the existence of a vibrant religious community and to a settlement that clearly shared South Arabian characteristics.

Though Yeha predates Axum, the Axumite Empire is the earliest state structure to leave significant evidence of its existence in Ethiopia. With its roots in the pre-Christian era, over various periods Axum encompassed lands on both sides of the Red Sea and had significant trade and cultural links with Egypt, Ancient Greece, as well as the Persian and Indian empires.

The historical record documenting the language of the early Axumites indicates use of what has been termed Sabaean writing form, similar to the script used by civilizations that flourished in what is today the Yemen. Alongside use of this Middle Eastern script, there are indications of the use of Greek, evidenced by inscriptions recording the victories of the Axumite kings, as well as on coins minted by the ancient monarchs. Parallel to the Greek and Sabaean forms, the Ge'ez alphabet, a uniquely Ethiopian script, emerged.

Alongside the development of an indigenous writing form, one unique to the African continent, visual art, music, and architecture also flourished. With the introduction of Christianity in the early fourth century, making Ethiopia one of the first states to embrace the new religion, a new era of ecclesiastical artistic expression dawned. A significant body of work survives to this day of iconographic paintings and illustrations in religious texts, a custom that also finds reflection in the brilliant frescoes and epic paintings that adorn the walls of Ethiopian Orthodox churches.

During this same period, Islam, the last of the great monotheistic religions, was born in the Middle East. Ethiopia was to play a critical role in Islam's struggle for continued existence and growth. When followers of the Prophet Mohammed met with severe persecution in Arabia and faced the possibility of total annihilation, the Prophet instructed them to cross the waters of the Red Sea to Ethiopia. There they would find a country that would be sympathetic to their cause and would give them refuge. Mohammed's followers made it to the court of the Ethiopian emperor, followed by emissaries of the Arabian powers with a message that the followers of the Prophet were outlaws who should be handed over for punishment.

Having heard the emissaries' request, the emperor turned to the followers of the Prophet to ask their reasons for fleeing their homeland. They described to him the nature of their persecution and the necessity of seeking refuge. He inquired about their religion and upon hearing their words recognized the shared monotheistic character of Christianity and Islam. He then questioned them on their knowledge of Jesus Christ and their response, based on Mohammed's teachings, endeared them to him. He told the Arabian emissaries to return to their countries, stating that even if they were to give him 'a mountain of gold', he would not surrender the disciples of Islam.

With the weakening of the polytheistic forces in Arabia, the refugees returned home to the task of establishing and spreading the Islamic faith. Due to this crucial assistance given to the fledgling religion, the Prophet Mohammed issued an injunction against the waging of Jihad, Islamic holy war, against Ethiopia (a call that has not always been faithfully followed). Islamic presence in Ethiopia dates to these early days – pointing out a remarkable fact about Ethiopia; Judaism, Christianity, and Islam all played important roles in the evolution of Ethiopia with traditions of all three continuing to form significant characteristics of Ethiopian society.

In the second half of the first millennium, Axum went into decline, a process marked by a significant contraction of lands under its control. This led to the concentration of the empire in the highland fastness of Ethiopia as the mountains provided natural barriers against invaders from the coast. A tremendous challenge to the power of the empire emerged during the tenth century in the form of an uprising led by the Jewish princess Yodit Gudit. Ethiopian lore holds that she sacked the town of Axum, destroyed churches, and that her followers pillaged the land. Nonetheless, the Orthodox Christian faith survived though Axum was subsequently succeeded by the Zagwe dynasty.

This new group of Christian emperors endowed Ethiopia with some of the most remarkable examples of human ingenuity in the world. In the twelfth century A.D., in the town of Lalibela, named after the most famous of their denizens, monolithic stone churches that survive to this day were carved out of the solid rock. UNESCO has designated Lalibela as a World Heritage Site, and the churches there are considered by many to be among the wonders of the world.

The Zagwe Dynasty lasted until the thirteenth century when, under the leadership of Yekune Amlak and with the support of the Orthodox Church, the Solomonic Dynasty was reinstated. In Ethiopian tradition, the history of the monarchy that survived till the late twentieth century begins in the tenth century B.C. with the visit of Makeda, the Queen of Sheba, to the court of King Solomon. Queen Makeda is said to have traveled to Jerusalem out of a desire to witness for herself the legendary wisdom of Solomon. While the queen indulged herself in questioning King Solomon he grew more and more enthralled with her beauty. The queen, however, rejected his advances until the frustrated king resorted to trickery. Solomon made her agree not to take anything that belonged to him without his consent, and that if she did she would have to sleep with him. The agreement made,

Solomon proceeded to have a very salty dinner prepared, a meal at which no water was served. That night, parched from the meal, the queen suffered severe discomfort. She left her chambers in search of water and finding a pitcher began to drink. Immediately the king confronted her saying she had violated the terms of their agreement. Though the queen insisted that it was only water, her pleas were to no avail. The result of their subsequent union was a son who ascended the Ethiopian throne as Menelik I, thereafter known as the first emperor of the Line of Solomon.

Upon becoming emperor, Menelik I visited his father in Jerusalem where he was accorded the Seal of Solomon, as well as a host of Levite priests, the first born sons of those serving in Jerusalem, to accompany him to Ethiopia. The priests supposedly stole the Ark of the Covenant from the temple in Jerusalem, only informing Emperor Menelik long after. Legend holds that Menelik, though initially angry at their deception, eventually accepted it was the will of God that the Ark was meant to travel to Ethiopia with him.

Following the conversion of the empire to Christianity, a church dedicated to St. Mary of Zion was built at Axum. It is believed that this is where the *Tabote Tsione* (Ark of the Covenant) is housed. A unique characteristic of the Ethiopian Orthodox Church is related to this belief that the Ark was entrusted to its care. Every Ethiopian Church has at least one tabot, a replica of the Ark, in its sanctuary. A church is considered but an empty shell without the presence of the tabot, the essential element that bestows religious significance to the physical structure of the church.

From 1270 onwards, criteria for ascending the Ethiopian throne were based on direct descent from the Solomonic Line. Over the ensuing centuries, the empire expanded and contracted in various stages. Lands on the Red Sea coast and to the east and south of the country that had been lost to Muslim principalities were retaken and absorbed into the empire. Expansion southward extended cultural and commercial links into lands that today form southern Ethiopia. Orthodox Christianity also spread south during this time, the most celebrated proselytizer being St. Tekle Haimanot.

In the 16th century, disaster struck in the form of an Islamic uprising led by Ahmed Ibn Ibrahim, popularly known as Ahmed Gragn (the left-handed). The dramatic civil war that ensued pitted Muslims against Christians. The war devastated Ethiopia and resulted in the destruction of many churches with their priceless repositories of treasures, manuscripts, and ecclesiastical items. The town of Lalibela, with its remarkable church structures, is said to have survived only because of Ahmed Gragn's awe and incredulity upon witnessing the marvel of their design.

Emperor Lebne Dengel sought assistance from Portugal to help contain the uprising. Following up on previous appeals by his mother, the Regent Empress Eleni, the request was a plea along religious lines requesting the assistance of fellow Christians against an Islamic threat. The belated arrival of Portuguese soldiers after the death of Emperor Lebne Dengel turned the tide and with the battlefield death of Ahmed Gragn the rebellion was ultimately crushed.

Cooperation with European co-religionists allowed the Christian Empire to withstand the threat of the Ahmed Gragn uprising. The experience was an important demonstration of Ethiopia's vulnerability against advances in military technology to which it had no access. Ahmed Gragn's relatively small fighting force, equipped with Turkish-supplied matchlock rifles, was able to easily devastate a standing army of several hundred thousand. Another important lesson was the benefit of enhanced ties with Christian Europe to withstand threats against the continued survival of a Christian state surrounded by Muslim potentates. This concern for maintaining the sovereignty of the Ethiopian Empire would become even more pronounced during subsequent centuries.

The arrival of Portuguese military support also brought the entry of Jesuit missionaries into Ethiopia. Jesuit proselytizing, particularly among the ruling class, ultimately led to the conversion of Emperor Susenyos, grandchild of Emperor Lebne Dengel, to Catholicism. Consequent attempts by him to impose Catholicism in Ethiopia led to further rebellion within the country, this time pitting Christian against Christian. This conflict finally ended with the abdication of Emperor Susenyos and the succession to the throne by his Orthodox Christian son, Emperor Fasiladas. Emperor Fasiladas immediately expelled the Jesuit mission to Ethiopia, restored the paramountcy of the Ethiopian Orthodox Church, and established the new capital of Ethiopia at Gondar.

Gondar's establishment in the 17th century witnessed a renaissance for the Ethiopian Empire. The rise of Gondar was marked by a resurgence in cultural vitality – most notably with the building of new churches and the unique castles that set it apart from the rest of Ethiopia. These structures have endowed Ethiopia with a remarkable heritage that continues to be celebrated until the present day.

The decline of Gondar in the 18th century as the center of the empire was marked by the emergence of the *Zemene Mesafint*, or Era of the Princes. In Ge'ez the term literally means 'era of the judges' in reference to the period directly following the Exodus when the Jewish people were ruled by wise leaders or 'judges'. In Ethiopia, this period was characterized by a steady weakening of the centralized state and a subsequent rise in prominence by regional fiefdoms. The emperor became largely symbolic. Real power shifted between the regional potentates, each vying for domination and control of the puppet emperor in Gondar. Outer edges of the empire operated almost independently of the center.

The weakening of the state after the Ahmed Gragn rebellion also facilitated the massive northward migration of the Oromo peoples from the south. The Oromo integrated into the empire in some parts and set up peripheral states in others. The demographic characteristics of the country changed dramatically, enriching the multi-cultural nature of Ethiopia, but also resulting in challenges of integration and the creation of a cohesive state unit.

By the middle of the eighteenth century, fragmented Ethiopia was facing increasing external threats from various directions – notably from the Sudanese border to the west, and from Turkish/Egyptian claims on the Red Sea coast. The divided nature of the empire rendered it virtually incapable of responding to these challenges until the rise of Emperor Tewodros in the middle of the nineteenth century. The rise to power of Tewodros, an emperor not of the Solomonic Dynasty, demonstrates the flexibility of Ethiopian imperial structures, particularly in the face of sheer force and military strength. Though Tewodros was to later claim descent from Solomon, that was a contested claim made in the interests of asserting absolute legitimacy. The *Zemene Mesafint* came to an end during his reign as he steadily subdued regional forces, sometimes with legendary brutality, in a bid to recreate a united Ethiopia.

Emperor Tewodros (1855-68) began the quest for modernization in Ethiopia, restructuring the state, military, and economy along lines that would allow the country to combat external threats. Tewodros recognized the necessity of acquiring European technology, particularly knowledge of modern weaponry, to achieve this aim. That ambition would ultimately lead to his untimely downfall.

Tewodros' objective was not just to import foreign arms – proving difficult to secure – but to establish centers for arms production within Ethiopia. With this in mind he requested the assistance of the government of Queen Victoria, believing quite naively that a fellow Christian monarch would come to his assistance in the mission of safeguarding his Christian Empire against encroachments by Muslim Egypt. However, Egypt being an important center for Britain in terms of trade and British investments, the British could find no compelling economic or political reasons to assist Tewodros. The entreaty by the emperor proved unsuccessful and the responses he received, or lack thereof, were not commensurate to the respect he believed his due as a fellow Christian monarch.

This, combined with his temperamental personality, led him to imprison the British mission to his court at his fortress capital, Meqdela. The emperor's harsh reaction elicited the famous response by Britain, who sent an expeditionary force led by Sir Robert Napier to secure the release of the prisoners. The force made its way from the Red Sea to Meqdela in record time, assisted along the way by Ethiopian chiefs who gladly collaborated against an individual they considered a brutal leader.

When his defeat became apparent, Tewodros released his prisoners and sent the British a peace offering in the form of a herd of cattle. The conciliatory gesture had no effect. Faced with defeat and the prospect of capture by British forces, Emperor Tewodros committed suicide – preferring to kill himself rather than face the indignity of capture. The British stormed the fortress capital and looted the contents. Members of the assembled force took these treasures back to Britain where they remain to this day.

By the time of Emperor Yohannes IV (1872-89), the indifference with which the British had treated Emperor Tewodros' requests for assistance evolved to unabashed duplicity as agreements entered into by treaty were reneged upon and abandoned. The rise of Mahdism in the Sudan, threatening British as well as Ethiopian interests, swiftly altered the dynamics of the region. Alliance with Ethiopia was now of strategic importance to the British and they subsequently signed a treaty with Emperor Yohannes IV.

Emperor Yohannes agreed to fight against the Mahdists and to facilitate the transfer of Egyptian troops across his territory. In return, Emperor Yohannes would reclaim the Bogos area (north and northeastern parts of present-day Eritrea) for Ethiopia, as well as secure free transit of goods and services through the port of Massawa. He fulfilled his side of the agreement completely; faithfully facilitating the transfer of Egyptian soldiers from the Mahdist surrounded fortresses in the Sudan.

Following the Berlin Conference of 1885 and the onslaught of the 'Scramble for Africa', Britain's main rival in Africa was France. In the Horn of Africa, France only had a beachhead in the territory of French Somaliland, the present-day state of Djibouti. The British were determined that France should not acquire the land being vacated by Egypt along the coast. Despite Emperor Yohannes' entreaties for access to the sea, requests based on historic claims and the needs of a modernizing state for port facilities, British avowals of alliance and friendship proved to be only pretensions. Emperor Yohannes and Ethiopia were betrayed as soon as the threats that had led Egypt and Britain to seek an alliance were contained. The British instead allowed and even encouraged the Italians to assume control of the strategic Red Sea port of Massawa.

In 1889, Emperor Yohannes died of wounds suffered in the Battle of Metemma during his heroic defense of the western frontier of Ethiopia. The Mahdist threat from the Sudan had resulted in the sacking of Gondar in 1888. Containing this threat to Ethiopian sovereignty was therefore of paramount importance and characterized the final days of his rule. While Yohannes was busy fighting this threat, Negus Menelik of Shoa continued expansion of the empire to the south, west, and east. With the death of Emperor Yohannes, Negus Menelik became Emperor Menelik II, and inherited an Ethiopia that was much larger, more centralized in terms of the emperor's power, and much stronger than it had been in over a century.

With the crowning of Emperor Menelik (1889–1913), the empire's center shifted to the region of Shoa, in what is today central Ethiopia. Menelik went far towards consolidating the unification process begun by Tewodros, and expanding the realm to the present day borders of Ethiopia. Peripheral kingdoms and sheikdoms were integrated into the empire, whether peacefully or through force.

One of the most significant events during the reign of Emperor Menelik was the Treaty of Wechale, signed with Italy in 1889. This treaty had two versions, one in Amharic, the other Italian. A key article in the Amharic version read that Italy would make available facilities for Ethiopian diplomacy and relations with other European powers should Ethiopia require such assistance. In the Italian version of the same clause, Ethiopia was obliged to go through Italy for all its foreign dealings, suggesting that Ethiopia had surrendered control of her foreign relations to Italy – in effect making Ethiopia a protectorate of Italy.

While Ethiopia protested and made repeated requests for correction of the text, Italy was using its interpretation of the treaty to make claims over Ethiopia in European capitals. Disagreement over this clause would ultimately lead to military confrontation.

Fighting between Ethiopia and Italy began in late 1895. By March of 1896, the colonial army of Italy, a mixed force of native Eritrean conscripts as well as Italian regulars, prepared for a showdown with the Ethiopian forces. The threat to Ethiopia's independence had the effect of galvanizing a truly national response and formerly feuding sub-national forces rallied around the emperor.

On St. George's Day, which in March 1896 fell on a Sunday, the Italians made the fatal decision of attacking. In their strategic calculations, attacking on a major saint's day, especially on the Sabbath when devout Orthodox Christians would be busy attending to religious observations and rituals, would be to their advantage. The Italians thought that the emperor and his entourage would be at prayer, and ill-prepared to withstand an attack.

Ras Alula, governor of the northern province of Tigray, was one of the military leaders under Menelik's command and had deployed spies to report on Italian movements providing Menelik's forces with a critical advantage. Although reports of enemy mobilization had become regular events the situation that Sunday was different. Reports of Italian movement were higher than usual and it was clear that this time there would be action. The church service that Menelik was attending was cut short and the bugle sounded. Fighting ensued, and by afternoon it was clear that a tremendous defeat had befallen the Italian army.

The Battle of Adwa is replete with awesome stories of bravery, patriotism, and heroism. St. George, the patron saint of the Ethiopian armed forces, is said to have fought alongside the Ethiopians. Legendary tales of military calculation and strategy abound including the heroic presence of Empress Taitu. The wife and personal advisor of Menelik, Taitu was renowned for her suspicion of foreigners and was a major influence toward abrogating the Treaty of Wechale. Empress Taitu, who had previously dealt a catastrophic blow to an enemy division by diverting their water supply, went out onto the battlefield and urged the men on before bowing down to the ground to pray for victory.

Adwa proved a resounding victory for Menelik and Ethiopia in many respects. The victory resulted in the uncontested legitimization of the centralized authority of the office of emperor under Menelik. If there were still any doubts that the *Zemene Mesafint* was over, Adwa banished them forever. Shoa became the undoubted center of Ethiopian power, recognized by all as the new seat of government to which they were subject.

With the northern borders quiet, Menelik was able to focus on expanding the reach of his authority to the south, southwest and east. Expansion halted where Emperor Menelik came up against the colonial powers. He subsequently entered into treaties with them leading to the definition of Ethiopia's present borders. These treaties were important checks on further colonial encroachment on Ethiopian territory.

Though Emperor Menelik maintained his main capital at Ankober, the seat of Shoan kings, scarcity of firewood necessitated moving the entire community to the Entoto hill range on the northern and western fringes of present-day Addis Ababa.

An imported resource that would play a critical role in the development of Addis Ababa made its debut during this period, namely eucalyptus, or *Bahir Zaf* (tree from across the ocean). The trees were planted around Entoto and fast replaced the denuded hillsides, making unnecessary another move to the settlement called Addis Alem.

Emperor Menelik first settled at this location in 1881 and in 1886 the settlement moved down the hills to the plains below. Empress Taitu orchestrated the descent, which allowed her easier access to the therapeutic hot springs. As the importation of eucalyptus trees had removed the primary reason for moving the capital, and foreign legations had already begun preparations for permanent settlements in the Entoto environs, by 1892 Emperor

Menelik was convinced to settle there permanently. Taitu renamed this site Addis Ababa (new flower) because of a unique flower which she is said to have discovered on the plains below Entoto.

The dawn of the modern age in Ethiopia occurs during the reign of Emperor Menelik, after the Adwa victory and with the establishment of Addis Ababa as the permanent capital of the empire. Among the major innovations introduced at this time were a modern currency and postage stamps bearing the Emperor's image and seal. The quest for access to port facilities led to the establishment of a joint venture between the imperial government and French interests in the form of the Railroad Company that laid the tracks that connect the Djibouti port with Addis Ababa. Although Emperor Menelik had passed away by the time it was completed in 1917, credit for its establishment belongs to him. The first automobile arrived in Ethiopia during the reign of Emperor Menelik, as did telephones, electricity, and the first telegraph system. This telegraph system was the foundation of the communications network that over the course of the century would link remote and otherwise inaccessible areas of the country with each other and the world beyond.

Emperor Menelik established the first modern education facility in the country, the Menelik II School. During his reign the first modern hospital was built in Harar by one of the emperor's trusted confidants and a hero from the battle of Adwa, Ras Mekonnen, governor of Harar and father of the future Emperor Haile Selassie. The number of Ethiopians visiting the outside world, including travelling abroad for education, also began to increase.

Emperor Menelik completed the foundation begun under Emperor Tewodros several decades previously; the foundation of a united and centralized empire which subsequent leaders would inherit and upon which they would build their legacy. The seeds for the ambitious and far-reaching changes that the ancient and conservative empire of Ethiopia would experience were all sown during Emperor Menelik's reign, and their ramifications are still being felt today.

NOVEMBER 1904 HARAR

TAFARI MAKONNEN, THE FUTURE EMPEROR, IN A PICTURE TAKEN BY A MISSIONARY IN HARAR, FOLLOWING TAFARI'S APPOINTMENT AS DEJAZMACH AT THE AGE OF THIRTEEN

BORN TO RULE

THE BATTLE OF ADWA WAS A PIVOTAL EXPERIENCE FOR ETHIOPIA, AS WELL AS FOR ALL PEOPLE OF AFRICAN DESCENT. ITALY'S DEFEAT BY AN ETHIOPIAN ARMY POSSESSING FAR INFERIOR TECHNOLOGY WAS AN UTTER SHOCK TO EUROPEAN IMPERIALISM. ETHIOPIA'S VICTORY AT ADWA DEMONSTRATED THAT ETHIOPIA WAS NO LONGER A DISPARATE AMALGAMATION OF WARRING AND DIVIDED POTENTATES, BUT THAT UNDER THE LEADERSHIP OF EMPEROR MENELIK IT HAD BECOME A UNITED STATE CAPABLE OF DEFENDING ITS INDEPENDENCE AGAINST A MODERN EUROPEAN POWER. MENELIK AND TAITU GRACED THE COVERS OF LEADING EUROPEAN MAGAZINES; THEIR EXPLOITS AND SUCCESSES MADE FRONT-PAGE NEWS IN MANY MAJOR NEWSPAPERS. THE GUARDIAN IN GREAT BRITAIN DECLARED ADWA TO BE THE MOST SIGNIFICANT VICTORY BY AFRICA OVER EUROPE SINCE THE TIME OF HANNIBAL.

As the undoubted under-dog in the entire affair, the sympathies of the average non-racist citizen of the world were with Ethiopia, and even in Italy the victory proved a major boon for enlightened members of the Italian intelligentsia opposed to the entire Italian imperialist project. There were marches and demonstrations in the streets of Rome and other Italian towns with protesters chanting 'Viva Menelik!'

The victory over Italy also had tremendous repercussions within Ethiopia. It was in effect the defining and galvanizing event that solidified the centralization begun by Emperor Tewodros. After over a century of a divided Ethiopia where regional chiefs and kings defied the power of the emperor, the Italian experience brought into harsh perspective the rapidly changing global context that threatened the survival of Ethiopia. Adwa demonstrated the need for a strong centralized state to withstand the threats of the day, and Emperor Menelik proved beyond any doubt his ability to lead and his status as uncontested head of the empire. Menelik's victory strengthened the office of emperor and this was part of the legacy that Emperor Haile Selassie was to inherit.

On 23 July 1892, Lij Teferi Mekonnen was born to Ras Mekonnen Welde Michael and Woizero Yeshimebet Ali, at their country home in a village called Ejersa Goro, approximately fifty-five kilometers outside of Harar Town.

Ras Mekonnen was the cousin of Emperor Menelik II, and a direct descendent of Negus Sahle Selassie of Shoa of the imperial Line of Solomon. Ras Mekonnen had played an active role during the campaign of Adwa, and served Menelik in a role that today would be considered the job of a foreign minister *(Autobiography I, 17)*. He was Emperor Menelik's closest and most trusted confidant. Indeed, until his untimely death in 1906, it was widely believed that the emperor would declare Ras Mekonnen his heir. This fact must have had great bearing on Teferi's later interest in and successful bid for the throne, particularly after Ras Mekonnen pronounced Lij Teferi his chosen successor in 1905 *(Marcus, 5)*.

Little is known about Lij Teferi's mother Woizero Yeshimebet Ali, daughter of a nobleman from Wollo *(Marcus, 3)*. She was the second wife of Ras Mekonnen and, as her name suggests, was possibly born Muslim. Woizero Yeshimebet had experienced several stillbirths while the rest of her children had all died young *(Mosley, 22)*. The birth of Lij Teferi was therefore a momentous occasion for the couple. He is said to have been born in the middle of a storm and that the heavy downpour was taken as an augury of fertility, good fortune, and success. Lij Teferi was Woizero Yeshimebet's only child to survive into adulthood. Eighteen months after his birth, at the end of a subsequent pregnancy, she passed away due to complications during childbirth.

At the time of Lij Teferi's birth, his father was the governor of Harar, an important region of Ethiopia that had previously existed as an autonomous city-state. Harar had been briefly occupied by Turkish and Egyptian forces penetrating inland from their holdings on the Gulf of Aden. Following the Egyptian retreat from Harar in the mid 1880s, the then Negus Menelik, along with his trusted cousin Ras Mekonnen, marched on the defiant city in 1887. They were successful in subduing the city and as a reward for his gallant service Ras Mekonnen was awarded the governorship of Harar province. This was an important region as, through its links with ports on the Gulf of Aden, Harar Town was a vital center for trade between the Ethiopian interior and the outside world.

Despite the fighting to subdue Harar, Ras Mekonnen endeared himself to the region's people through the respect he demonstrated toward the Muslim traditions of the residents and the charismatic nature of his dealings with the multicultural communities in his new territory. In late 1895, when he sent out the call to arms to fight against the Italians, he was able to recruit a loyal army from the population around Harar, and together they would lodge some of the greatest victories of that campaign.

Ras Mekonnen was Emperor Menelik's most trusted ally in the otherwise contentious domestic political scene. In 1890, Emperor Menelik sent Ras Mekonnen to Italy as his personal envoy to sign supplemental articles to the 1889 Wechale Treaty. The trip to Europe had a tremendous impact on Ras Mekonnen, as it provided a revealing perspective on the backwardness of his home. He returned convinced of the importance of a modern education, a belief that was to have great implications for his son.

In 1902, Ras Mekonnen made his second trip abroad, this time to attend the coronation of King Edward VII of Great Britain. Again, the exposure to Europe reinforced his desire for modernization in Ethiopia. Upon returning from this trip, Ras Mekonnen was pleasantly surprised to find that his son had become fluent in French. He reported this to the emperor who instructed his favorite cousin to bring his child prodigy to Addis Ababa so that he could witness Lij Teferi's proficiency for himself. Father and son made the long journey to Addis Ababa, Lij Teferi's first major trip outside Harar.

At the court of Emperor Menelik, Lij Teferi proved his mastery of the French language in a visit that launched a special relationship between the reigning monarch and the young boy destined one day to inherit the seat of power *(Mosley, 40)*. Two years later, at the age of twelve, Lij Teferi was awarded the rank of Dejazmach and appointed governor of Gara Muleta district in Harar Province. With his new rank, Dejazmach Teferi was assigned a separate household complete with full staff, and was invited to sit in on official meetings and banquets with the 'great officers', even proffering his advice and opinions on matters under discussion *(Autobiography I, 21)*.

One year later, while traveling from Harar to Addis Ababa, Ras Mekonnen fell ill with typhoid forcing him to cut his journey short. He retired with his entourage to the Kulubi area near Harar town where he convalesced. Ras Mekonnen was not to recover and, when it became clear that the end was near, he summoned Dejazmach Teferi to his bedside. During these last days, Ras Mekonnen wrote to Emperor Menelik entrusting his favorite son to his care *(Marcus, 6)*. Ras Mekonnen passed away at dawn on 21 March 1906 *(Marcus, 6)*.

The death of Ras Mekonnen was a great relief to the various aspirants to the throne. Among these was the Empress Taitu, who was fond of neither Ras Mekonnen nor Dejazmach Teferi *(Mosley, 41)*. As she was arranging for her nephew Ras Gugsa to marry Menelik's daughter Zawditu, Taitu hoped to see Zawditu ascend the throne. Through the couple, whom she intended to influence and dominate, Empress Taitu would have continued exercising power and kept the critical role she had played in guiding the development of Ethiopia. Another contender for the throne was Lij Iyassu, Emperor Menelik's grandson and the son of the powerful Ras Michael of Wollo. With Ras Mekonnen out of the picture, these two camps became the main contenders for the throne.

A major decision to be made following the death of Ras Mekonnen was the question of who should assume the governorship of Harar. Under the influence of Empress Taitu, Menelik was convinced that Dejazmach Teferi's older half-brother Dejazmach Yilma was the fitter of the two to govern Harar. Empress Taitu's plotting was further influenced by the fact that Dejazmach Yilma was married to her niece Woizero Asselefech. *(Auto I, 25)* Menelik acquiesced but at the same time summoned Dejazmach Teferi to Addis Ababa for safeguarding, in accordance with his obligations to Ras Mekonnen. Menelik's decision must have been a great disappointment for Dejazmach Teferi who had even had his own governor's seal designed in anticipation of his new position *(Marcus, 7)*. Dejazmach Teferi was instead made governor of Selale District to which he sent a representative to govern on his behalf while he enrolled at the Menelik II School.

Besides his traditional schooling, the court of Emperor Menelik provided the young Dejazmach Teferi with an intimate hands-on education in the ceremonies and rituals of court life. Dejazmach Teferi was able to observe firsthand the successful monarch and study his style of rule. These lessons proved an invaluable experience that he would draw on when he became emperor. An important lesson learnt was regarding all the intrigue and scheming that characterized imperial politics, and the means by which the monarch used these rivalries among his courtiers to keep himself informed and in control.

In 1906, Emperor Menelik suffered the first of a series of strokes, marking the start of a slow deterioration in his mental capabilities and ability to govern. The question of succession emerged as an urgent issue, providing ripe conditions for the hatching of plots and counter plots as all prepared themselves for the emperor's death.

The question of succession was also of interest to Britain, France, and Italy. Each had colonies bordering Ethiopia and considered various sections of Ethiopia as being within their zone of interest. Anticipating a return to infighting and instability upon Emperor Menelik's death, in 1906 the colonial powers signed a tripartite agreement carving Ethiopia into their prearranged spheres of interest. Although nominally declaring respect for Ethiopia's sovereignty, the agreement was drawn up without consulting the Emperor and presented to him as a *fait accompli*. If the opportunity had arisen, this agreement would have been the basis upon which the colonial powers would have divided the country. Although the agreement halted colonial power rivalry within Ethiopia, a boon for domestic stability, it would later be used by the Italian dictator Mussolini to justify invading Ethiopia.

During his stay in Addis Ababa, the bonds between Dejazmach Teferi and Emperor Menelik grew steadily stronger. Supposedly, Dejazmach Teferi's quiet demeanor, his remarkable patience, and his clever and astute thinking fascinated the Emperor. Menelik's obvious feelings toward Dejazmach Teferi did not endear the latter to other members of the palace.

From an early age on, there was a marked rivalry between Lij Iyassu and the young Teferi. On one occasion, while out riding on the hills around the palace, Dejazmach Teferi's horse stepped into a rabbit hole, throwing him off its back. Lij Iyassu is said to have laughed at the mishap, urging the court minstrel to come up with rhymes ridiculing Teferi. Dejazmach Teferi made no reaction but instead remounted his horse and challenged Lij Iyassu to a race.

He not only won the race but also continued to display great feats of horsemanship, clearly out-performing Lij Iyassu. Later it was discovered that he had a broken wrist *(Mosley, 52).*

In April 1908, Dejazmach Teferi was appointed governor of Darrassa, Sidamo Province *(Marcus, 10).* The time he spent as governor of Sidamo was a special period in the future emperor's life. In his autobiography, Emperor Haile Selassie wrote, "During the period I served in my governorate of Sidamo, I had a time of perfect joy" *(Autobiography I, 29).* For the first time he was responsible for administering a large population. As governor he was involved in matters relating to taxation, judicial affairs, and general administration. Sidamo was an important learning experience and an opportunity to enact some of the modernizing changes he felt necessary for Ethiopia.

Dejazmach Teferi spent one year in Sidamo before events in Addis Ababa compelled his return. Emperor Menelik had suffered another stroke, this time rendering him too ill to govern. He finally proclaimed his grandson Lij Iyassu his heir and successor to the throne and the following year Ras Bitwodded Tessema Nadew was pronounced Regent. This was a tremendous blow for Empress Taitu who was hoping that her stepdaughter would succeed.

As Menelik's deterioration reduced his capacity to rule, two camps emerged at court with Empress Taitu on the one hand attempting to retain power, and the emperor's ministers who wanted to have Lij Iyassu immediately crowned on the other *(Marcus, 11).* In a demonstration of his astute political skills, Dejazmach Teferi refused to join either faction, instead appearing to remain on the sidelines. This had the effect of both currying favor with the empress and also keeping him safe from the ministers and nobles. On 3 March 1910 a proclamation by Empress Taitu appointed Dejazmach Teferi governor of Harar *(Autobiography I, 32).* A few days later the ministers orchestrated a coup against the empress declaring all her appointments void with the single exception of Dejazmach Teferi's governorship *(Autobiography I, 32).* The regency of Ras Bitwodded Tessema ensued.

At this point it was rumored that monks had seen a 'dream-vision' in which they were told that Dejazmach Teferi's governorship of Harar did not bode well for Lij Iyassu's government *(Autobiography I, 35).* Concerned about the omen, Ras Bitwodded Tessema had Lij Iyassu and Dejazmach Teferi swear an oath that as long as Lij Iyassu behaved honorably towards Dejazmach Teferi and did not threaten his governorship Dejazmach Teferi in turn "would not seek, by trickery or rivalry, Lij Iyassu's throne" *(Autobiography I, 35).*

While in Addis Ababa, Dejazmach Teferi met and instantly fell in love with Woizero Menen (granddaughter of Ras Michael, niece of Lij Iyassu), who was hiding from her husband, Ras Lul Seged *(Mosley, 68).* Soon Dejazmach Teferi and his fiancée traveled together to Harar where arrangements were made for her divorce from the Ras. On 31 July 1911, Dejazmach Teferi and Woizero Menen were united in marriage *(Autobiography I, 42).*

On 10 April 1911, Ras Bitwodded Tessema suffered a massive stroke, and passed away (*Thesiger*, 45). As news of his death spread, the regional chiefs gathered in Addis Ababa for what seemed a showdown over who would be declared regent. Ultimately, Lij Iyassu, with the support of Fitawrari Habte Giorghis, Emperor Menelik's War Minister, took over the palace and asserted his preeminence. He would serve as de facto leader of Ethiopia until the death of Emperor Menelik *(Thesiger, 46).* From 1911 onwards, the situation turned increasingly chaotic as the order and centralization achieved by Emperor Menelik was cast aside by the debauchery and brutality of Lij Iyassu. Allegedly, these traits were encouraged by various elements in the palace, including Empress Taitu, who sought to use alcohol and women to influence him. Effective central government in Ethiopia virtually disappeared.

With Menelik's death in 1913, Empress Taitu's influence in Addis Ababa came to an end. Suspicious of her Gondar heritage and leanings, the predominantly Shoan Council of Ministers, in a rare moment when their interests coincided with Lij Iyassu's, orchestrated her banishment to Entoto.

Ethiopia was fortunate in this period that World War I kept the European powers otherwise occupied and relatively disinterested in East Africa. Under Lij Iyassu's rule it would have been relatively easy for any of the colonial powers that had historically demonstrated interest in gaining control of Ethiopian territory to achieve their goals. The reign of Lij Iyassu brought Ethiopia very close to disintegration as his eccentricities and inability to consolidate centralized power led to revolts in various parts of the country. The hard-fought-for national union achieved by Emperor Menelik was under serious threat. It seemed that only the region of Harar was content with the return of the native-born Dejazmach Teferi. In both Sidamo and Harar, Dejazmach Teferi put into practice what amounted to a revolutionary form of governance, marked by improvements in the treatment of peasants, and in the land tenure and taxation systems. At this point in his career, Dejazmach Teferi was considered by others, as well as by himself, to be an anti-feudal activist.

Meanwhile, the situation with Lij Iyassu was growing progressively worse as he openly demonstrated complete disregard for both the old nobility and the customs and traditions of conservative Orthodox Christian Ethiopia. As described by Emperor Haile Selassie, following the death of Ras Bitwodded Tessema Nadew, Lij Iyassu "sought in everything the company and counsel of worthless men who only wanted their immediate profit, while the great nobles and ministers became hostile and removed their hearts from him" *(Autobiography 1, 44)*.

Lij Iyassu spent increasing amounts of time away from his capital, instead roaming the Danakil plains, going on at least one slave raid in Gimira, and engaging in unseemly behavior. His absence from Addis Ababa facilitated the development of stories defaming his character, including tales of mass slaughter, rape, as well as a depraved craving for blood *(Thesiger, 47)*. As unrest mounted, his association with Islam provided the conservative Orthodox Christian nobility with a pretext for orchestrating his removal from power.

To his credit, Lij Iyassu recognized that Muslim communities, who represented a significant portion of the Ethiopian population, were indeed treated as second-class citizens by the powerful Christian establishment. In a sense, Lij Iyassu's clear desire to redress some of the inequalities and injustices perpetrated in the name of religion was visionary and commendable. However, accomplishing such a feat of diplomacy would have required political skills that he did not possess. (One of the major developments in twentieth century Ethiopian history has been the rapprochement of the two ancient religions. Today, the peaceful and respectful coexistence of the two religions is one of the celebrated and unique characteristics of Ethiopia.)

During World War I, Lij Iyassu demonstrated pronounced leanings toward support of the Turkish/German alliance. This brought the British, French, and Italian legations in Ethiopia against him, a reversal from previous years when they had endorsed his rule. In Harar, the Turkish Consul Mr. Ydlibi, operating with the support of Lij Iyassu, was accused of supporting Seyyid Muhammed Abdullah (the Mad Mullah as the British referred to him) who was fighting the British and Italians for the independence of Somalia. By 1914, Lij Iyassu had removed the Ogaden region from Dejazmach Teferi's control, handing it over to Abdullai Sadik, openly described by the British Minister, Wilfred Thesiger, as 'a notorious Harar Arab' *(Mosley, 78)*. Lij Iyassu is said to have been lured into the Central Powers' camp

1917 LOCATION UNKNOWN

DEJAZMACH TEFARI AND HIS HEIR ASFA WOSSEN, THE FUTURE CROWN PRINCE

through Sadik's influence, believing that they would help him unite the Muslim peoples of Ethiopia, Eritrea, and Sudan into one great Islamic empire.

The relationship between Dejazmach Teferi and Lij Iyassu continued to deteriorate. In 1915, Lij Iyassu traveled to Harar where his close connections with Islamic leaders again became evident. Although the reports about his behavior and his growing antipathy towards the Orthodox Church had led to strained feelings on the part of Dejazmach Teferi towards his cousin, he still felt bound by his oath of loyalty. Subsequent events would alter matters.

On 7 June 1915, Dejazmach Teferi and a small entourage accompanied Woizero Menen as far as Lake Alamaya just outside Harar as she set off for Addis Ababa to attend her brother's funeral. The group camped on the lakeshore and proceeded to go for a boat ride. While on the lake, the boat on which Dejazmach Teferi, his cousin the future Ras Imru, their former tutor Abba Samuel, and several other companions were relaxing, began to fill with water and eventually sank. Unable to swim ashore, most of the boaters drowned. Dejazmach Teferi himself was close to drowning and was only saved by Abba Samuel who kept his head above water until rescuers arrived. In his autobiography, Emperor Haile Selassie wrote, "having just escaped death ... Our soul had barely been prevented from getting separated from our body, but we were unable to recognize anyone or to speak" *(Autobiography 1, 43)*. Having saved his protégé's life, the exhausted Abba Samuel slipped under water and drowned *(Marcus, 16)*.

According to some accounts, a servant in Harar later confessed to having been paid by Lij Iyassu's attendants to sabotage the boat, drilling a hole in it and covering it up with mud so that it would gradually wash away while the boat was on water *(Mosley, 81)*. Abba Samuel had been a tremendous influence on Dejazmach Teferi and the suspicion that Lij Iyassu might have had a hand in the accident that caused his mentor's death further eroded the bonds placed on Dejazmach Teferi by his oath.

In May 1916, Lij Iyassu summoned Dejazmach Teferi to Addis Ababa *(Autobiography I, 45)*. While in Addis Ababa Dejazmach Teferi consulted with the Council of Ministers over the country's rapidly deteriorating security situation and reports that Lij Iyassu was considering an alliance between Ethiopia and the Ottoman Empire. After consultations, the Council dispatched a note to Lij Iyassu demanding the removal of Sadik from governorship of the Ogaden and that he sever relations with the Mad Mullah. There was no reaction from Lij Iyassu. Meanwhile Woizero Menen gave birth to a boy, an heir to Dejazmach Teferi. At this point Dejazmach Teferi was placed under virtual house arrest, ordered by Lij Iyassu not to move from the capital. As Dejazmach Teferi had too many supporters in the capital for Lij Iyassu to dare move directly against him, Iyassu instead slipped out of the capital himself and headed for Harar with an old enemy of Dejazmach Teferi, Woizero Menen's previous husband Ras Lul Seged *(Mosley, 86-90)*.

Dejazmach Teferi had left his family in the safe hands of his trusted cousin and lifelong friend, the future Ras Imru, and was able to appraise his family of the impending danger. Warned about the approaching threat, Woizero Menen disguised herself as a Harari woman and together with her children, was smuggled out of Harar. When Lij Iyassu and Ras Lul Seged stormed Dejazmach Teferi's residence in Harar, his wife and newly born heir were long gone *(Mosley, 90)*.

On 17 August 1916, Lij Iyassu sent a letter to Dejazmach Teferi informing him that he had been removed from the governorship of Harar. This act, along with the invasion of his household, released Dejazmach Teferi from his oath of loyalty to Lij Iyassu, allowing him to take on the leading role against Lij Iyassu that the Shoan nobility had been begging for him to assume. Fearing that his life was in danger from pro-Iyassu forces, upon his family's arrival in Addis Ababa Dejazmach Teferi promptly arranged for his heir to be placed in the protective care of the British Minister *(Thesiger, 50)*.

In Addis Ababa, Dejazmach Teferi embarked upon the task of uniting the entire Council of Ministers, not just the Shoan contingent, against Lij Iyassu; a mission in which he succeeded. Lij Iyassu's seizure of predominantly Muslim Harar, where he courted Islamic leaders and was photographed wearing Muslim attire, was taken as further proof of his association with Islam and alienation from the Church. Attempts were made to persuade Abuna Mattewos, head of the Orthodox Church in Ethiopia, to declare Lij Iyassu excommunicated from the church and all citizens of Ethiopia free of all oaths of allegiance to him. Although Abuna Mattewos was hesitant about declaring the excommunication, sentiment was clearly against Lij Iyassu and, despite his lack of canonical authority, the Etchege, head of Ethiopian monasteries and second to the Abuna in the church hierarchy, declared Lij Iyassu and his followers excommunicated *(Marcus, 19)*.

Dejazmach Teferi was only able to gather support from the nobility with the promise that he was not attempting to assume power for himself, for while they were all united against Lij Iyassu they were also suspicious of Dejazmach Teferi who they saw as a serious threat to their traditional interests. Instead, Emperor Menelik's daughter Zawditu was selected to succeed, with Dejazmach Teferi simultaneously made regent and heir. Though the initial proclamations referred to Teferi only as heir, he began exercising power immediately, taking over prerogatives from the queen, making him in effect regent to the much older monarch *(Bahru, 129)*.

The father of Lij Iyassu, who had been crowned Negus Michael of Wollo and Tigray by Lij Iyassu following the death of Emperor Menelik, rallied his forces to defend the honor and position of his deposed son. However, his attempt to regain the throne for Lij Iyassu by force was to prove unsuccessful. Negus Michael assembled a considerable army and began marching towards Addis Ababa. The Shoans assembled a force under Ras Lul Seged (who had switched loyalties against Lij Iyassu) and met him in battle. Negus Michael was victorious and Ras Lul Seged was among the casualties. The government forces, led by Fitawrari Habte Giorghis and joined by a unit led by Dejazmach Teferi himself, rallied again and at the Battle of Sagale on October 27, Negus Michael's forces were defeated and the Negus was captured. The throne was firmly secured in the hands of Woizero Zawditu and Dejazmach Teferi. Dejazmach Teferi followed up his victory at the Battle of Sagale with a remarkable display of magnanimity, a trait that would repeat itself on several auspicious moments during his long reign as emperor. Declaring that 'we are all Ethiopians', he went on to pardon tens of thousands of Negus Michael's soldiers, allowing them to return home unharmed *(Marcus, 24)*. The turn of events in favor of Woizero Zawditu for a short while appeared to be a success for Empress Taitu, who at this point returned to Addis Ababa from her exile atop Entoto. Her nephew Ras Gugsa was finally married to Woizero Zawditu and Empress Taitu was closely allied to the Minister of War Fitawrari Habte Giorghis, a member of the old guard put in that position to counter the modernizing influence of Ras Teferi. The old empress believed the situation to favor her and anticipated a return to power brokering. This was not to be as in the person of Teferi, Empress Taitu was to discover a schemer and strategist more sophisticated and successful than herself.

Shortly after the deposition of Lij Iyassu, the now Ras Teferi threw a huge banquet in honor of the Dowager Empress, Woizero Zawditu, and her husband Ras Gugsa. The gathering was seemingly innocuous the deception at hand perfectly disguised in feasting and celebration.

As the two men indulged in drink and food and the evening grew merrier the two empresses retired to their quarters, quite satisfied that they could now remove the isolated Ras Teferi and assume all power for themselves.

On 11 February 1917, Woizero Zawditu was crowned Empress of Ethiopia and Ras Teferi declared heir to the throne and regent of the empire. The event, described by an observer as "a gorgeous ... spectacle", was the first coronation ever attended by European dignitaries *(Marcus, 26)*. The event impressed the visiting dignitaries, as well as the masses of Ethiopians who had gathered in the capital from all over the country. It would also be a valuable rehearsal for Ras Teferi's coronation thirteen years later.

During the years 1916-1917, Ras Teferi began establishing the necessary support structure required for his successful rule and necessary for implementation of his ambitious reform agenda. In line with the unifying and centralizing trends instituted by Emperor Menelik, Ras Teferi recognized the critical role that Addis Ababa would play in the future of the empire. It was natural therefore that his first political appointments would be to positions in the city government and the central province of Shoa. He appointed Heruy Wolde Selassie, who would later serve as foreign minister, director of the municipality; Tekle Wolde Hawariat became the chief clerk of Addis Ababa, responsible for taxation and administration; and Kassa Hailu was made Ras and governor of Shoa *(Marcus, 28)*. The selections were indicative of the direction that the country would take under Ras Teferi's leadership. The first two were well educated, progressive, and loyal to the regent while the new governor of Shoa appreciated the rising challenge facing Ethiopia from European imperialism, and the critical need for change to withstand these forces *(Marcus, 28)*. According to Harold Marcus, one of the more authoritative biographers of Emperor Haile Selassie, "from the very beginning Tafari outlined the nature of his rule: he would concentrate on Addis Ababa, Shewa, and foreign affairs, around which he would construct a centralized state" *(Marcus, 28)*.

A salient characteristic of the new agents of the state, the 'Young Ethiopians', was their generally humble non-aristocratic origins and their education. Capability would become the requirement for political position which was no longer to be the exclusive prerogative of the nobility. This had the effect of pitching this new class up against the nobility – a state of affairs that guaranteed the Young Ethiopians' loyalty to their patron, Ras Teferi. The Young Ethiopians held the promise of at last modernizing and developing the ancient empire.

Although with the coronation of Empress Zawditu a major milestone had been crossed, both for the country and the future emperor, things were far from stable. Rebellions broke out in the north of the country among chiefs and warlords unwilling to submit to Empress Zawditu's rule. Furthermore, Lij Iyassu, who was still at large, entered into partnership with rebellious factions from Wollo province led by Ras Yimer. Following a prolonged standoff, fighting ensued during the rainy season. By this time the government forces were better equipped than the rebels, and what ensued was a rout. Although Lij Iyassu escaped, he would no longer be a serious threat to Ras Teferi.

In Addis Ababa, Empress Zawditu and Empress Taitu continued plotting against Ras Teferi, though without success, and in late 1917 Empress Taitu finally passed away. After recovering from a serious bout of influenza, the so-called Spanish Flu of 1918 that killed tens of thousands in Addis Ababa and throughout the country *(Marcus, 37)*, Ras Teferi emerged stronger than ever before.

Ras Teferi came to power at a critical juncture in Ethiopian history. Ethiopia was one of the last bastions of independence in Africa and therefore a natural target for colonization, particularly for the latecomer to the colonial race, the recently unified nation-state of Italy. Defeat at Adwa and Emperor Menelik's subsequent moves to unify Ethiopian territory had temporarily stopped threats from outside. However, the postwar period in Europe would witness the rise of new political forces that would eventually place the sovereignty of Ethiopia under renewed and ever greater risk.

Ras Teferi now found himself in a position to begin the reforms and developments that he had long imagined and desired for Ethiopia. Events in 1918 would result in the dissolution of the Council of Ministers, further strengthening Ras Teferi's ruling hand. Growing urban dissatisfaction due to unemployment and the wrath of unpaid soldiers, who had served in the campaigns against northern rebellions, resulted in the forming of a military council, that demanded payment from the Council of Ministers. People assumed that the empty government coffers were due to corruption and when the Council failed to respond, the military council immediately insisted on its dismissal. The threat of riots and continuing disruption of public order forced the empress to accede to the military's demands *(Marcus, 33-34)*. The urban crisis in Addis Ababa continued into 1919 with confrontations between the conservatives, led by Fitawrari Habte Giorghis, and Ras Teferi's progressive camp. Ras Teferi emerged triumphantly with executive powers after Empress Zawditu intervened between Ras Teferi and Fitawrari Habte Giorghis, selecting Ras Teferi because he possessed the required vision, energy, and ability to deal with the modern realities of the day *(Marcus, 46)*.

One of the first foreign policy moves attempted by Ras Teferi was to have Ethiopia enter into World War One on the side of the Allies. The proposed alliance, wherein Ethiopia would join the fight against Turkey in Arabia, would be in return for modern armaments, as well as a place at the peace treaty for Ethiopia at the end of hostilities. The Allies, however, considered Ethiopia too weak to be of much assistance in their war effort, and Ras Teferi's proposal was dismissed. The Allies also feared that allowing Ethiopia access to modern weaponry would result in old stock being traded, filtering into, and destabilizing the neighboring colonies *(Marcus, 29)*. Furthermore, the colonial powers, particularly Italy, were opposed to a militarily powerful Ethiopia, especially as Italy was still nursing hopes of reversing the Adwa defeat and acquiring Ethiopian territory.

The Great Powers were doubtful of Ras Teferi's capability to unite Ethiopia. Despite this skepticism, Ras Teferi was able to make significant headway in uniting the country and moving ahead with his development agenda.

In 1923, after securing agreements from the governors to back him by fulfilling any reform measures that might be required of Ethiopia, Ras Teferi applied for Ethiopia's admittance into the League of Nations. However, the road to acceptance was far from smooth. A whole host of spurious issues were raised by detractors, with regard to Ethiopia's qualifications for membership.

Among the concerns voiced were doubts regarding Addis Ababa's control over the entire country and the ability of Ras Teferi's government to retain power. The existence of slavery, a characteristic of Ethiopian society at the time, was another major concern. Ras Teferi embarked on a public relations crusade to combat the anti-Ethiopian campaigns launched by such institutions as the Anti-Slavery and Aborigines Protection Society in Great Britain. A 1918 ban on slavery was reinforced in 1922 with a general order to all governors to ban the slave trade.

Ras Teferi had prepared extensively prior to the final submission of the Ethiopian application in August 1923. When London and Rome responded negatively to the bid by Ethiopia, Ras Teferi cabled both governments, who, surprised by the unexpectedly strong response, instructed their delegations in Geneva to relax the conditions as long as Ethiopia committed to working towards the total elimination of slavery. Ethiopia's bid passed, as both Italy and Great Britain wanted to maintain as positive relations as possible with the Addis Ababa government so as to defend their interests; Great Britain on Lake Tana and the Nile waters, and Italy with respect to her desire for a greater Italian colony in East Africa *(Marcus, 54)*.

Opposition to Ethiopia's membership to the League of Nations also came from domestic sources, namely the entrenched nobility who saw the move as putting Ethiopia in danger of being overrun by foreigners. Additionally, as the abolishment of slavery directly affected the economic interests of the aristocracy, it would take some time before the promulgation went into effect, as the nobles were reluctant to let go of their source of labor. On the other hand, as a bitter emperor was to later recall, the anticipated national security benefits of membership were welcomed. "There was great joy in Addis Ababa," Emperor Haile Selassie wrote, "... for no other reason other than that We thought that the Covenant of the League would protect us from the sort of attack which Italy has now launched against us" (Autobiography *I, 77)*.

The anti-slavery proclamation was followed up by the Weapons Control Edict of 19 April 1924, designed to control and limit arms imports. It was another measure intended to impress upon Europe that the government in Addis Ababa was taking the necessary measures to maintain control over the security situation in Ethiopia.

In 1922, Ras Teferi made another dramatic break from long-standing tradition by traveling abroad – the first time that an Ethiopian emperor or heir to the throne had left his country. This first journey was across the Red Sea to Aden where, during a Royal Air Force air show he was to experience his first ride in an airplane. The experience so impressed him that Ras Teferi expressed his ideas for an Ethiopian air program *(Marcus, 50)* – an idea ridiculed by Europeans because of Ethiopia's poverty and backwardness. Several decades later, despite continuing poverty and backwardness, Ethiopia, under Emperor Haile Selassie, developed a successful commercial airliner, (Ethiopian Airlines), as well as an air force. In 1922, the military advantage of air power was immediately apparent to Ras Teferi, especially its potential use for domestic power consolidation purposes, and upon his return to Ethiopia he immediately declared the importation of airplanes into Ethiopia illegal except under his strict orders *(Mosley, 129)*.

1924 JERUSALEM

seated center: RAS TEFERI VISIT OF RAS TEFERI, THEN THE REGENT AND HEIR APPARENT, TO JERUSALEM
SEATED WITH HIM ARE ETHIOPIAN OFFICIALS WHO ACCOMPANIED HIM TO JERUSALEM AND
AN UNIDENTIFIED TURKISH GROUP

THE JAWS OF A LION

IN 1924, RAS TEFERI RECEIVED INVITATIONS FROM THE GOVERNMENTS OF PALESTINE, EGYPT, GREECE, ITALY, FRANCE, GREAT BRITAIN, GERMANY, AND BELGIUM FOR OFFICIAL STATE VISITS. THE PROPOSED TRIP AND THE PROLONGED ABSENCE THAT IT WOULD ENTAIL FROM ADDIS ABABA INITIALLY RAISED CONCERN AMONG THE NOBILITY. EVENTUALLY, RAS TEFERI CONVINCED THEM OF THE ADVANTAGES TO BE GAINED FROM MAKING THE TOUR. REGARDING HIS MOTIVATIONS FOR GOING ON THE TRIP HE LATER EXPLAINED, "I HAD THE HOPE AND CONVICTION THAT MY JOURNEY TO EUROPE WOULD GIVE ME THREE BENEFITS: 1) TO SEE WITH MY OWN EYES EUROPEAN CIVILIZATION AND THE BEAUTY OF THE CITIES OF PARIS, LONDON, ROME, BRUSSELS, ATHENS, AND CAIRO ABOUT WHICH I HAD READ IN BOOKS, FIRST AT SCHOOL AND LATER IN OFFICE; 2) WHEN RETURNING TO MY COUNTRY AFTER MY VISIT TO EUROPE, I THOUGHT IT WOULD BE POSSIBLE TO INITIATE SOME ASPECTS OF CIVILIZATION I HAD OBSERVED WITH MY OWN EYES, ALTHOUGH IT WOULD BE IMPOSSIBLE TO CARRY THIS OUT ALL AT ONCE AND IN FULL; 3) TO FIND A SEA-PORT; PRIOR TO OUR JOURNEY WE HAD RECEIVED SOME ENCOURAGEMENT FROM FRANCE AND ITALY AS REGARDS ACCESS TO THE SEA" *(Autobiography I, 83)*.

Ras Teferi set off on the extensive tour accompanied by his wife, and an entourage that included potential rivals that might have used his absence to usurp power.

On 16 April 1924, Ras Teferi and his group left Addis Ababa for Djibouti. Four days later they boarded the boat that would take them to the Suez Canal and the al-Kantara 'bridge', from where they boarded a train for Jerusalem *(Autobiography I, 85)*. The travelers celebrated Easter in Jerusalem and went on to visit various holy sites *(Autobiography I, 85)*. Back in Jerusalem discussions were held with officials regarding securing the Ethiopian sanctuary there.

The entourage departed from Jerusalem on 1 May 1924, traveling to Cairo where they were received 'with honour' by King Fuad *(Autobiography I, 88)*. The next day was spent with the Coptic Patriarch Abuna Querillos to whom Ras Teferi presented a variety of gifts including a golden crown, a golden cross, a golden staff, a silk tunic embroidered with gold, and a cape *(Autobiography, 88)*.

The group's departure from Alexandria for France was accompanied by a cannon salute. Such demonstrations of respect, to be repeated at the various ports visited along the route of the tour, impressed Ras Teferi so much that he would later recount each occasion in full detail in his autobiography.

The first stop in France was at the port of Marseilles where the mayor and high government officials met them. Ras Teferi was treated to a tour of French warships docked at Marseilles, and as he would later write, "We saw the strength of the construction and the size of the guns and then returned greatly impressed" *(Autobiography I, 90)*. On 16 May they left for Paris where President M. Millerend, Prime Minister M. Poincaré, Marshal Foch, the mayor of Paris, and various important ministers met them. Ras Teferi presented a splendid spectacle wearing jodhpurs and a white cape which was decorated with a medallion of the Order of Solomon *(Marcus, 62)*.

Ras Teferi held meetings with Prime Minister Poincaré and officials of the French Foreign Ministry regarding acquiring Ethiopian access to the Red Sea through the French Protectorate of Djibouti. The other item on the agenda was possible improvements to the Klobukowski Accord, which granted foreigners in Ethiopia undue immunity from Ethiopian law. The French representative in Addis Ababa had indicated that it might be possible to arrange a deal with regard to Djibouti. However the response to Ethiopian queries in Paris was vacillatory. Ras Teferi attempted to convince the French by suggesting that Italy had promised similar port access at Assab. However, he would come away from the discussions empty-handed and disappointed

During the official part of their visit to Paris, the Ethiopian entourage stayed in the Quai d'Orsay, the palace of the French Foreign Ministry. Afterwards, Ras Teferi rented a villa in Paris that would serve as the base for the travelers. At the 'Villa Camasterand' Ethiopian students studying in France came to visit the group. Among them was the future Ras Andargachew Messai, husband of Emperor Haile Selassie's daughter, Princess Tenagne Worq. He made a speech welcoming the regent to France in which he testified to the significance of Ras Teferi's on-going tour: "Your arrival has made the name of Ethiopia heard all over the world ... Ethiopia has the duty to thank you, for her joy is not only for the present moment but will be lastingly transmitted from generation to generation" *(Autobiography 1, 93)*.

The rented villa in Paris was used as a staging ground for visits to the other capitals where Ras Teferi had been invited. Ras Teferi visited Brussels at the invitation of King Albert. From Brussels he traveled to Luxembourg where the Grand Duchess Charlotte, who had extended the invitation to him, gave birth on the day of his arrival. Ras Teferi was hosted by the Grand-Duchess' husband, Duke Felix of Bourbon-Parma, whom he told that "it would remain in Our heart as a remembrance of joy that on the day of Our arrival in Luxembourg the Grand-Duchess should give birth to a male child" *(Autobiography 1, 95)*. From Luxembourg Ras Teferi returned to Paris via Brussels and soon after set out for Sweden by way of Amsterdam, Rotterdam, and Hamburg. In Sweden, the Archbishop of Uppsala hosted him, before he met with the king at his seaside palace outside of Stockholm *(Autobiography 1, 97)*. On 14 June he returned to Paris.

Two days later, Ras Teferi set off for Rome. At the Italian border he boarded the royal train on which he traveled the rest of the way to Rome where he was met by King Victor Emmanuel and the Italian dictator Benito Mussolini. The public response in Rome was energetic and memorable as the crowds yelled "Long live Italy! Long live Ethiopia! Long live His Highness Crown Prince Tafari!" Reflecting on the trip while in exile and with Ethiopia under Italian occupation, Emperor Haile Selassie would write, "when they think of this today, how extraordinary must this appear to them?!" *(Autobiography 1, 98).*

While in Rome, Ras Teferi pursued prospects of acquiring a free zone for Ethiopia at Assab. The response from Mussolini and his Director of Political Affairs was a draft treaty granting the concession, but at the same time rendering Ethiopia a protectorate of Italy *(Marcus, 65).* Taken aback at the complete rejection of the Ethiopian plan, Ras Teferi diplomatically informed the Italian Government that he would present the draft agreement to the Council in Addis Ababa, knowing full well that it would never gain acceptance. After meeting with the Pope he returned to Paris.

On 7 July, Ras Teferi and his group left Paris for England. They were escorted by two warships on leaving the French coast and were greeted at Dover by a 21-gun salute. In London, the Crown Prince of Great Britain greeted the future emperor. However, the racist King George had to be pressured by the Foreign Office into entertaining the imperial guest *(Marcus, 66).* Unlike their monarch, the British public and press were captivated by Ras Teferi.

In London, Ras Teferi met with Prime Minister Ramsay Macdonald regarding border disputes, as well as the British desire to build a dam on Lake Tana. By building the dam Britain hoped to regulate the flow of water into the Nile so that excess water from the rainy seasons could be stored and released for use down river during the dry season. Ras Teferi was resolved to maintain Ethiopia's right to independent action on this matter. However, the strategic importance of Lake Tana for Britain's dependencies down river would keep British sights on acquiring damming rights, even at the expense of Ethiopian sovereignty.

During his discussions with the Prime Minister, Ras Teferi raised the issue of the arms embargo imposed on Ethiopia by the Great Powers, in particular the 1919 arms control agreement signed by Britain, France and Italy, and further restrictions that had been imposed in 1923 *(Autobiography 1, 107)*. The talks were to no avail as the Prime Minister insisted that any decision regarding such matters had to be made in consultation with France and Italy. Ras Teferi also brought up the subject of acquiring access to the sea through British Somaliland. He explained that "the entire object of the Ethiopian Government for the future is to get very close to foreign countries by undertaking the tasks of civilization." In order to achieve this he insisted that a port was necessary adding, "if the British Government were to give the Ethiopian Government a sea-port as patrimony, there would be eternal and unshakable friendship" *(Autobiography 1, 108)*. The British Government was not inclined to be so generous or accommodating.

As the entourage prepared to leave, King George presented Ras Teferi with one of the looted crowns from Meqdala explaining that "as a constant memorial of your visit to London and of your meeting with us, we are returning to you the crown of Emperor Theodore which the commander of the British army at the time of the Magdala campaign had brought back" *(Autobiography 1, 109)*. The British were returning to Ethiopia as a gift what they had stolen almost six decades earlier, and to add insult to injury, the crown that was returned was the inferior of two crowns that had been taken from Meqdala. The other, more valuable, crown remains in Great Britain to this day.

On 28 July, Ras Teferi left London for Paris. While in Paris Ras Teferi placed orders for the new Menelik I medal to be struck, as well as for the Menelik II statue which would later be mounted in front of St. George Cathedral in Addis Ababa on the day before his coronation as emperor. New stamps were also ordered in Paris bearing the images of Empress Zawditu and Ras Teferi *(Autobiography, 115)*. The entourage departed France on the 15th of August for their next stop, Greece.

Pomp and ceremony, as had been the case throughout the trip, marked the official welcome to Greece. As the boat that they were traveling in approached the Greek port of Piraeus, they were accompanied by airplanes and honored by a warship gun salute. On the 21st of August they departed Athens heading back to Cairo where discussions continued regarding securing an Ethiopian chapel in Jerusalem. The regent left an envoy to continue the discussions as it became time to return home. The entourage departed Suez on 27 August arriving in Djibouti on the 31st. Four days later, Ras Teferi was back in Addis Ababa, arriving just before the Ethiopian New Year.

The visit to Europe endeared the Crown Prince to the public in all the countries that he visited. His charm and pleasant demeanor, as well as the spectacle of an independent African prince claiming descent from Solomon and Sheba and heir to the throne of a country that had recently defeated a European army made him fascinating to the European public. As explained by Harold Marcus in his biography of Emperor Haile Selassie, "Westerners steeped in contemporary racial stereotypes had always found Tafari's features, manners, wit and intelligence gratifyingly non-African" *(Marcus, 58)*. For Ras Teferi the tour, similar to the experience of his father before him, revealed the true extent of Ethiopia's backwardness and the immense steps that had to be taken for Ethiopia to successfully move into the modern era as swiftly as possible.

Almost immediately upon returning from his travels, Ras Teferi ordered the building of a new institution of learning, the Teferi Mekonnen School which was built across the street from his palace. The school opened in May 1925, and was an auspicious addition to the education program initiated by his great predecessor Emperor Menelik II. The establishment of schools would become an important legacy of the Haile Selassie era. In 1931, he would convince the Empress Menen to establish a school for girls bearing her name *(Sandford, 48)*. Using his own resources Ras Teferi also had a new hospital built opposite his then palace, inaugurated as the Betesaida Hospital, later renamed Haile Selassie I Hospital, and subsequent to the Ethiopian Revolution of 1974 known as the Yekatit 12 Hospital. Another major development of the time was the launching of *Berhanena Selam* weekly newspaper in 1924, the country's first periodical (Ras Teferi had imported two printing presses in 1921-22). *Berhanena Selam* would prove a valuable propaganda tool, used with remarkable success to promote the views and agenda of its founder. Under the Mahra Tibeb Press the *Aymero* weekly paper made its debut. Income from the printing houses was reserved for the Betesaida Hospital *(Autobiography I, 63)*.

Despite the public relations success for Ethiopia and himself, Ras Teferi was unable to secure one of his main objectives during the tour; acquiring Ethiopian access to the sea. Back in Addis Ababa the Council rejected the offer that had been put forward by Italy. The trip did, however, help in influencing France toward lifting the arms embargo against Ethiopia as a way of restoring French prestige in Addis Ababa following their rejection of Ethiopia's requests for free access to the sea in Djibouti *(Marcus, 71)*. In 1925, Ras Teferi lobbied the League of Nations regarding Ethiopia's rights to import arms as a sovereign and equal partner in the world body. Previously, the League of Nations had declared the entire continent of Africa a 'prohibited zone'. With French support, Ethiopia gained exemption from this embargo and immediately placed orders for arms from Belgium, Switzerland, and

Czechoslovakia. Meanwhile, temporarily frustrated, Great Britain involved itself in looking for new ways to prevent Ethiopian access to weapons *(Marcus, 72)*.

As proudly outlined in Emperor Haile Selassie's autobiography, auspiciously titled *My Life and Ethiopia's Progress*, his list of accomplishments during the regency period were quite remarkable. They stand out because he was starting from almost nothing, and no Ethiopian leader before him, or since, has been able to boast of so many 'firsts'.

During the 1920s, the number of cars, trucks, motor cycles and bicycles in Ethiopia increased dramatically precipitating an urgent need to build a network of paved roads for both the capital and the provinces. Work began on these roads so that by the time of the Italian occupation in 1935 "districts that could previously be reached in ten or fifteen days can now be reached in two or three days" *(Autobiography, 76)*. The number of hospitals increased, not only in Addis Ababa, but also in the provincial capitals and major towns. A military college was set up in 1919 and, under the auspices of Prince Mekonnen, the duke of Harar, the Ethiopian Boy Scouts Movement was established "so that boys should carry out their duties well" *(Autobiography I, 70)*. Several generations of Ethiopian boys were to benefit from participating in the Boy Scouts movement until their dissolution following the 1974 revolution.

In 1927, Ethiopia's first national anthem was composed, along with a military march entitled '*March Teferi*' *(Autobiography, 70)*. At the same time, Ras Teferi went about securing the independence of the banking system by buying back the Bank of Abyssinia, previously set up through the Bank of Egypt, and transforming it into the Bank of Ethiopia. Ethiopia's first airplanes were purchased and on the diplomatic front, Ethiopia's first legations abroad were opened in various cities *(Autobiography I, 72)*.

1916 LOCATION UNKNOWN

PORTRAIT OF DEJAZMACH TEFERI THOUGH HE WAS APPOINTED DEJAZMACH AT THE AGE OF 13

THIS IS THE FIRST PORTRAIT IN FULL REGALIA

While moving forward with his modernizing agenda, Ras Teferi continued the process of consolidating his power, eliminating threats to his eventual coronation, and strengthening the centralized nature of the state. In 1926, Fitawrari Habte Giorghis, the old Minister of War, passed away. Ras Teferi moved fast before Empress Zawditu could take control of the late Fitawrari's land and holdings, effectively taking over the former minister's power for himself. He subsequently appointed a new Minister of War who would be loyal to him, as well as a new finance minister *(Marcus, 79)*. That same year the archconservative Abuna Mattewos, another reactionary force opposed to Ras Teferi's reforms, also passed away. Ras Teferi arranged for five Ethiopian bishops to be ordained in Alexandria, paving the way for eventual consecration of an indigenous Abuna, or Archbishop, and the Ethiopian Orthodox Church achieving independence from the Egyptian Church.

Between 1926 and 1928, Ras Teferi would reap the financial rewards of his reforms, particularly from the South where the new administrative structures and tax collection methods meant increasing funds coming to Addis Ababa. Trade with the outside world doubled during this period, with India and Japan becoming the major source of imports, while the United States became the major buyer of Ethiopian agricultural products. Trade agreements were also underway with additional countries, including Austria and the Netherlands *(Marcus, 80-86)*. These were deliberate measures designed to break Ethiopia's dependence on her colonial neighbors Britain, France, and Italy. However, their diminishing share in Ethiopia's trade would have negative repercussions for Ethiopian sovereignty. France, in particular, saw her share in trade decline significantly resulting in her removing previous support for Ethiopia in her foreign relations, especially with regard to the Anglo-Italian designs to carve up Ethiopia, an ominous prelude to the French offer of an Italian free hand in Ethiopia in 1935 *(Marcus, 86)*.

In 1927, the Italian duke of Abruzzi visited Addis Ababa and held talks with Ras Teferi regarding the construction of a road from Assab to Dessie, as well as providing Ethiopia port facilities at Assab. A treaty of friendship between Italy and Ethiopia, guaranteeing peace between the two countries for at least twenty years, was negotiated during the visit and signed the following year *(Autobiography, 147)*. The treaty was welcomed in Addis Ababa as it was believed that peace offered Ethiopia the best chances of developing quickly.

Also in 1927, Ras Teferi summoned the various rases to Addis Ababa for feasts where they were to renew their loyalties to him *(Mosley, 144)*. Most of the rases, having accepted Ras Teferi's paramountcy, traveled to Addis Ababa to make their supplications with the notable exception of Dejazmach Balcha of Sidamo. Repeated calls for him to appear in Addis Ababa were either ignored or flatly turned down. Finally, following the arrival of a strongly worded dictate Dejazmach Balcha set out for the capital with a huge following of several thousand men-at-arms. He set up camp in his own compound in Addis Ababa, from which he was invited to dinner at the Palace.

Dejazmach Balcha, correctly anticipating foul play, responded to the invitation with a query if he could bring some of his men *(Mosley, 145)*. Informed that his men would be treated as the honored guests of Ras Teferi he agreed to attend, warning the six hundred or so men that he chose to accompany him not to get too drunk and to remain alert against any possible treachery. The group was subsequently treated to a lavish meal with lots of honey mead. They were allowed to brag of their might and prowess – Ras Teferi stopping his own men from responding to the *fukera* (gregarious boasting of ones strength and ability to destroy any opponent with impunity). Finally Dejazmach Balcha and his men were bidden farewell and they made their way back to their own compound feeling confident that their display of might had cowed Ras Teferi into submission *(Mosley, 146)*.

However, a great surprise awaited them for when they arrived at Dejazmach Balcha's compound, the great encampment he had brought with him was nowhere to be seen. Apparently, while he and his 600 men were at the palace feasting, Ras Teferi had arranged for the rest of Dejazmach Balcha's men to be either bribed or threatened to disband, which they had proceeded to do up to the last man *(Mosley, 147)*. Dejazmach Balcha, recognizing that he had been outsmarted and defeated, released the rest of his men and sought refuge at St. Raguel Church on Entoto with the Etchege, the highest-ranking Ethiopian member of the Church. Ras Teferi subsequently had his forces surround both the church and the residence of the Etchege on Entoto.

Dejazmach Balcha was removed from office, accused of 'maltreating' peasants in Sidamo and conspiring against Ras Teferi *(Autobiography I, 153)*. The defeated Ras Balcha is said to have declared, "do not under-estimate the power of Teferi. He creeps like a mouse but he has jaws like a lion" *(Mosley, 148)*. This incident was very helpful to Ras Teferi as it served two purposes. Placing Dejazmach Balcha, who ended up living a life as a monk until the Italian invasion of 1935, under house arrest eliminated a threat. It also prevented the Etchege from meeting and influencing the newly arrived Abuna until Ras Teferi had been ensured of the Abuna's unwavering loyalty.

The Dejazmach Balcha incident was followed by a unanimous declaration by ministers, nobles, army commanders, and "all men holding office" that Ras Teferi should be made Negus *(Autobiography I, 154)*. Their request read, "May it please you to have H.H. Crown Prince Taferi proclaimed king and have him carry out, on his sole authority, any government business without having to consult anyone" *(Autobiography I, 154)*. The empress' immediate response was to request time to consider the proposal, and according to his autobiography Ras Teferi suggested that the request be removed, as it was irregular to have a king and an empress residing in the same city at the same time. The future emperor recorded that the crowds gathered outside the palace insisted and Empress Zawditu was compelled to agree. On 7 October 1928, Ras Teferi was crowned Negus *(Autobiography 1, 154)*. His new position as Negus was a clear sign to the whole country that his position as heir to the throne was indeed incontestable.

By 1929, most of the rases had declared their loyalty to Negus Teferi with the exception of Ras Gugsa, the former husband of Empress Zawditu. The periodic droughts that plague Ethiopia returned in 1928-29 accompanied by swarms of locusts. Starvation ensued in the north and at the same time provincial and local government officials insisted that peasants continue to pay taxes. The result was the eruption of revolts, social unrest and the development of a major political crisis *(Marcus, 93)*.

According to Negus Teferi's extensive spy network, Ras Gugsa was conniving to overthrow him with the support of Ras Hailu Tekle Haimanot of Gojam, Ras Seyoum of Tigray, and Sultan Abu Jaffer of Wollo. Negus Teferi requested that Ras Gugsa attack the rebellious Raya and Azebu peoples in Tigray, a ploy that turned against him when Ras Gugsa instead sought their support in a bid to topple Negus Teferi *(Marcus, 94)*. Religion once again provided the mandate for the rebellion, Ras Gugsa convincing his followers that Teferi intended to impose European civilization on Ethiopia, had converted to Catholicism, and was in the process of subverting the nation's ancient religion *(Autobiography 1, 158)*.

To contain this new threat Negus Teferi engaged in his usual strategizing. He bought off Ras Hailu and Ras Seyoum, but ensured that this fact was concealed from Ras Gugsa who would not know that he was alone until it was too late *(Mosley, 163)*. Negus Teferi, realizing the importance of having a professional army trained in modern military techniques, equipped with modern arms and loyal to him at the center of power, had enlisted the support of advisors from Belgium. This new modern army equipped with armored vehicles would take part in the fight with remarkable success, vindicating Negus Teferi's often-controversial policy of embracing foreign technology and advisers. The ensuing battle demonstrated Negus Teferi's newly acquired capability of successfully conducting a war without traditional leadership at the front *(Marcus, 95)*. Ras Gugsa's demise was coordinated from Addis Ababa. Negus Teferi had recently purchased four airplanes delivered complete with a pilot, the Frenchman Maillet, to fly the mini air force. Maillet tracked the course of Ras Gugsa's movements who never realized that the aircraft allowed his opponent to compromise his position, eventually facilitating his complete surrounding and defeat.

Ras Gugsa died on the 31st of March 1930 effectively dashing all hopes that Empress Zawditu might have had of escaping her barren and symbolic role as empress. She passed away two days later without hearing the news of her king's victory and husband's death. The Empress had contracted paratyphoid fever which, combined with her diabetic condition and the effects of the rigorous Ethiopian Orthodox Lenten fast, had weakened her severely. As her condition became critical, a priest advised "emergency dunking in Holy Water as a last resort" *(Marcus, 95)*. The ailing Empress Zawditu lapsed into a coma before dying in the early afternoon of 2 April 1930.

Her death closed a long chapter of scheming and plotting by Negus Teferi to ascend the throne, though the convenient timing of her death, two days after the death of her husband Ras Gugsa, led many to speculate that Negus Teferi might have poisoned her. A Council of State met on 2 April where Negus Teferi was unanimously declared the next *Neguse Negest*. He accepted, quoting Psalm 151 of the Ethiopian Orthodox Bible regarding the choice of David to be king of Israel over his older brothers *(Marcus, 96)*. On 3 April 1930, Ras Teferi announced the death of the Empress and that he had assumed supreme control. Despite the custom of crowning the new emperor before announcing that the previous monarch had passed away, Emperor Haile Selassie's coronation was postponed to allow time for invitations to be sent to foreign dignitaries as well as for appropriate arrangements to be made for the ceremonies. Following the customary period of mourning, the coronation was scheduled and preparations began immediately for an occasion Negus Teferi was determined would be a world class event designed to overwhelm his subjects and confirm to the world that Ethiopia was determined to take her place among the family of nations.

LATE 1940S ADDIS ABABA

STATE PORTRAIT OF THE EMPEROR

THE EMPEROR

ON 3 APRIL 1930, RAS TEFERI ANNOUNCED TO THE CITIZENS OF ETHIOPIA THAT EMPRESS ZAWDITU HAD PASSED AWAY. THE OFFICIAL STATEMENT READ:

'Proclamation in the name of the Crown Prince and Regent Plenipotentiary of the Ethiopian Realm, His Majesty King Teferi Mekonnen, on his ascending the Imperial Throne with the name of His Majesty Haile Selassie the First, King of Kings of Ethiopia. PROCLAMATION. In accordance with the Proclamation which our Creator abiding in His people, and electing us, did cause to be made, we have lived without breach of our Covenant as mother and son. Now, in that by law and commandment of God, none that is human may avoid return to earth, Her Majesty the Empress, after a few days of sickness, has departed this life. The passing of Her Majesty the Empress is grievous for myself and for the whole of the Empire. Since it is the long-standing custom that when a King, the Shepherd of his people, shall die, a King replaces him, I being upon the seat of David to which I was betrothed, will, by Gods' charity, watch over you'.

'Trader, trade! Farmer, plough! I shall govern you by the law and ordinance that has come to me, handed down from my fathers.' *(Mosley, 163).*

Subsequent events would show, however, that the laws and ordinances by which Emperor Haile Selassie I would govern were about to undergo drastic changes, as would many other aspects of life in the empire.

Emperor Haile Selassie I has the unique position of being what many have called the architect of modern day Ethiopia. Much of what defines Ethiopia today was put in place during his reign. It is through his vision and leadership that Ethiopia finally emerged from centuries of isolation and began to cautiously open up to the rest of the world.

With the death of Empress Zawditu, Ras Teferi finally arrived at the pinnacle of the Ethiopian power structure, the position of *Neguse Negest*, King of Kings. Preparations for the coronation began immediately with one of the more urgent tasks being to put a pleasant façade on the ramshackle town that Addis Ababa had developed into. Screens were put up to hide the slum areas that had evolved in various quarters. The fledgling police force was issued new khaki uniforms. The existing hotels were refurbished and new accommodations were built for the anticipated guests.

The 1930 coronation was a momentous occasion in the life of the nation, an event that almost seventy years later has yet to be matched in pomp and ceremony. For Emperor Haile Selassie it was the attainment of what he believed his destiny, a position for which he had been in preparation since his early childhood.

From the time he was a little boy, Lij Teferi was decidedly different from other children. Looking at photographs from his early childhood one cannot help but notice the serious demeanor – the knowledgeable, wise, and sage like expression that looks so lonesome on the face of a young boy. One can sense more than pride, and perhaps an element of awareness of the grave responsibilities that he was born to shoulder.

He grew up receiving an education that was probably unique at that time as only a handful of Ethiopians would have received such exposure to new languages and new thoughts, new knowledge about the world and the innovations radically altering the way that it works. It was an education that encompassed and superseded the knowledge imparted by traditional educators from the church, a fact that set him apart from his contemporaries. Most children of the nobility who had the means of acquiring a private tutor and modern education lacked the interest. Those few Ethiopians who did take advantage of the opportunity to receive a modern education, either did so abroad in environments completely removed from their Ethiopian traditions, or else were totally immersed in the life of missionary boarding schools where Ethiopian traditions and customs were not an immediate reality. Lij Teferi, on the other hand, was not only educated in the European system, but also had that education preceded and accompanied by a traditional Ethiopian church education. Chroniclers of the time indicate that when Dejazmach Teferi Mekonnen joined Menelik II School, his aptitude and level of learning far exceeded those of the regular students, requiring a special study program to be devised just for him. Most importantly, he was to learn the art of governance and statecraft, enriched by hands-on experience in the manners of the court.

The untimely passing of Ras Mekonnen had seemed to end Dejazmach Teferi's chances of becoming emperor. Had his father been named heir and succeeded Emperor Menelik it would have been a much simpler progression to power, but he might not have been the same type of ruler. There were vital repercussions to his becoming an orphan at such a young age, principally because it led to him living in a setting filled with competition, conspiracy and danger; the perfect, and perhaps only, place to learn the skills required to dominate the traditional political system. The defeat of Ras Gugsa was in a way the final test of his skill and proof of his capability to rule, to dominate and subjugate the Ethiopian polity. This achievement was rewarded several days later by the death of the sickly Empress and the nation-wide announcement that he was the new *Neguse Negest.*

The coronation was designed to make a huge impression on both the domestic public and the world at large. Haile Selassie wanted to demonstrate to the nobility and to his subjects across the land that under his leadership a new era, to be characterized by modernity and international respectability, had dawned for Ethiopia. He also wanted to make his coronation an absolute statement of the incontestable legitimacy of his ascension to the throne of the ancient Line of Solomon. The presence of a large contingent of foreign dignitaries was an important and calculated effect, which among other things was intended to impress upon the minds of the nobility that the international community was united in recognizing him as the new ruler of Ethiopia. The detail to ceremony and ritual was designed to dazzle his subjects while exhibiting the rich and ancient culture of Ethiopia to the world. The event was to be testimony that Ethiopia was fast emerging as a modern state fully deserving of an equal place among the civilized nations of the world.

An important group of invitees to the coronation was the world press. The media attention lavished upon Ras Teferi and his entourage during their 1924 tour had been an important lesson in the public relations benefit of good press coverage. The international press invited to the coronation, it was assumed, would report to the world the commendable developments that were occurring in Ethiopia. Journalists that had gathered in Addis Ababa were treated with special care and attention. The emperor even prepared a separate banquet exclusively for them *(Talbot, 28)*. Unfortunately for the emperor, however, the media coverage that Ethiopia, the coronation, and his own person received was not the glowing reports he had anticipated. Despite attempts to clean up the city, the poverty was clear to all. This apparent backwardness of the country was included in the published reports.

Ras Teferi's European tour had exposed him to the glitter and pomp of European courts. Traveling in Europe he had witnessed the products of the age of innovation, the technological advancements which were making machines like automobiles standard items of modern living. Among his major purchases during that tour were several vehicles.

Back in Addis Ababa the number of roads suitable for automobile use were extremely few. As a result, one of the major activities personally supervised by Ras Teferi from the time of his tour till the death of Empress Zawditu was the construction of roads. While significant progress had been made in this regard, Ethiopia's first asphalt road was laid down specifically for the upcoming coronation. It was upon this road that the imperial state coach, specially brought from Germany for the occasion, would travel.

Other imported items for the festivities included a marching band from England. The British also sent two scepters with inscriptions in Amharic. The French arrived with a Farman airplane, and the Italian representative, the prince of Udini, added another airplane, a Breda. In light of later events it is ironic that Mussolini, not yet the archenemy of Emperor Haile Selassie and Ethiopia, added a tank *(Mockler, 12)*.

Foreign nobility were put up at the palace and mansions fixed up for this purpose, while the remaining entourages of foreign guests either camped out in tents at their various legations, or found lodging in the city's hotels.

The traditional venue for the coronation of Ethiopia's emperors is the spiritual headquarters of the Ethiopian Orthodox Church at Axum. Although Emperor Haile Selassie did not travel to Axum for his coronation, the spiritual and religious detail accorded his coronation was certainly impressive. Forty-nine Orthodox priests and monks were brought to Addis Ababa from various parts of the country for the sole purpose of praying over and blessing the ceremonial garments that would be worn by the emperor and empress on the day of the coronation. For one week before the event, they took shifts praying continuously without stop until the coronation day, Sunday 2 November 1930 *(Talbot, 26)*.

The soon to be emperor and empress spent the night at the St. George Cathedral in prayer and spiritual preparation for the following day. Just after 7 a.m. the actual coronation ceremony began with the imperial family, members of the nobility, and the foreign dignitaries assembled in solemn observation. Emperor Haile Selassie took his oath and received his holy annointment, following which the Empress was crowned. The Abuna then made his exhortation to the gathered princes and nobility, as well as to the subjects of the empire at large, reminding them of their obligations and duties as subjects and citizens, binding them to be loyal and obedient to the emperor, charges that in the ancient traditions of Ethiopia included the threat of excommunication should they be violated.

The entire ceremony was marked by the ultimate in Ethiopian pomp and pageantry. Addis Ababa was overflowing with visitors from all parts of the country. The various nobles had brought with them huge entourages; all of them encamped on the hills and plains around the city. The event had also attracted many of the regular citizens of Ethiopia who travelled to Addis Ababa to be a part of the celebrations. Following all the religious ceremonies, the marching band from England put on an exhilarating show, and there were ululations and demonstrations of affection and endearment from the throngs that lined the streets hoping to catch a glimpse of the new rulers as their coach passed by.

The mixture between the old and time tested traditions of Ethiopia, as represented by the elaborate religious ceremonies that accompanied the coronation, and the modern elements imported from Europe, became the defining characteristic of the coronation, symbolic of the changes to come during the reign of the new emperor. The day after the coronation the newly crowned couple visited all the churches in the capital, giving thanks for the tremendous milestone that they had just passed, before retiring to their palace and the continuation of festivities. They would be modernizers, and at the same time, as monarchs inheriting the ancient traditions of Ethiopia, they would safeguard the heritage and customs of which they were now guardians.

Emperor Haile Selassie I had taken command of a country that had experienced debilitating disunity and fragmentation during the past century. At the time of his coronation Ethiopia appeared to be the most united it had been in centuries. Yet, there still remained salient characteristics of the traditional power structures that continued to present challenges for the emperor. The hereditary nobility, despite recognizing Emperor Haile Selassie's ascension to the throne, expected to maintain a certain degree of autonomy in their regional centers of power. The presiding cultural attitudes, especially when it came to power, were still very much defined by traditions inherited from the time of the *Zemene Mesafint*. The notion of achieving ultimate power by force had yet to be removed from the nobility's psyche. For Emperor Haile Selassie the task of consolidating power was not over.

The biggest threat to the new emperor came from Ras Hailu who governed Gojam as a semi-autonomous fiefdom. Ras Hailu, as well as Ras Seyoum of Tigray, expected that the new emperor would reward them for their complicity in his moves to eliminate the threat posed by Ras Gugsa earlier that year. One of their basic expectations was that at least he would confer upon them the rank of Negus.

Instead, Haile Selassie, in his first major act as emperor, issued Ethiopia's first constitution. The Constitution and the opening of Parliament were intended as a statement regarding the direction in which the new emperor intended to take Ethiopia. The Constitution reinforced the messages from the coronation indicating to his subjects that a new era had dawned for Ethiopia. For the outside world, the new constitution was further evidence of Ethiopia's progress under the leadership of the now Emperor Haile Selassie.

With patience and careful timing the young Dejazmach Teferi had climbed up the ranks of power until he attained the supreme position of emperor. Following this achievement, he moved with stunning speed to consolidate his position and protect it from all threats and menaces. The main issues that he addressed in the new constitution were concerned with the ever-contentious problems associated with succession. The other remarkable significant concerned the rights and obligations of the emperor. The new law severely curtailed many of the powers previously enjoyed by the hereditary nobility, concentrating them instead in the hands of the emperor.

These were fundamental and far-reaching measures that completed the process of centralization begun by Emperor Tewodros. Time and again in the course of Ethiopian history, the ability of regional chiefs to enter into alliance with foreign powers had seriously undermined the unity of the country as well as the power of the emperor by exposing the country to foreign manipulation. The 1931 Constitution was an attempt to end these divisions and create a truly united country.

The signing of the constitution itself became an opportunity to undermine the influence and power of the nobility. Less than a year had passed since the coronation festivities when the regional chiefs were once again summoned to Addis Ababa to witness the signing of the constitution, to ratify the document, and to observe the inauguration of the new parliament. Once in Addis Ababa the rases found to their great consternation that they were prevented from returning to their various regions for a period of six months. In the meantime a retinue of new bureaucrats, the product of the education program carefully attended to by Emperor Haile Selassie during the twenties, went out to the various regional capitals where they established the structures that would fully integrate the previously autonomous and semi-autonomous states into the centralized framework.

The whole affair was a well calculated severing of power of the nobility, in effect reducing them to mere messengers and expediters of the emperor's desires who were no longer free to rule their regions as they willed. The moves clearly strengthened the center, placing absolute power in the person of the emperor at the expense of the nobles *(Bahru, 140)*.

The new laws of succession, to which much of the new constitution was dedicated, explicitly stated that only descendants of Emperor Haile Selassie I could ascend the throne. This again marked a drastic departure from previous custom where being of the Line of Solomon was enough to be eligible for the throne. While the new constitution did indeed take care of old concerns regarding the smooth succession of power by putting in place detailed formula for how it should proceed, it is a bitter irony that these articles would never be invoked as the basis for succession to Emperor Haile Selassie.

Among the other prerogatives that became the exclusive preserve of the emperor were the right to grant titles, an absolute right of final decision on matters of justice, and also the exclusive right to declare war, raise and define the size and nature of the army. The right to confer land and estates also became the province of the emperor.

The constitution set forth the rules and regulations for the first parliament of Ethiopia. Although the conditions governing the first parliament could hardly be called democratic, for that period in Ethiopian history it too was a radically new feature of the political scene in Ethiopia, nominally designed to facilitate the development of participatory government. Absolute control ultimately rested with the emperor. However, the parliamentary system with its two houses, the Senate, made up of the hereditary nobility, and the Chamber of Deputies, made up of appointees by the hereditary nobility and the regional chiefs, whose members had to be of a certain education and/or position, represented another challenge to the authority of the hereditary nobility. Merit was introduced as one criterion for gaining power and position, which opened up the political scene to Ethiopians of all classes and background, who had the good fortune of going to school and proving their capabilities.

That Ethiopia did not have a 'constitution' prior to 1931 does not mean that there were no codified laws addressing issues of governance. The *Fetha Negest*, the Law of the Kings, evolved from the old legal traditions of Axum and the ancient civilizations of the Mediterranean, and was codified as the *Fetha Negest* during the Middle Ages. The *Fetha Negest*, as well as the laws of the Old Testament, had served as the guiding principles of government, law, and justice in Ethiopia for centuries.

During the early 1930s, the emperor and the small intelligentsia emerging in Ethiopia were grappling with the immense task of how to modernize a traditional society – how effectively to bring about what amounts to revolutionary change in a society whose roots were buried under centuries of history and tradition. The Ethiopia they had inherited possessed a conservative culture, which was removed from other cultures of the world, and isolated from the advances and developments other parts of the world were experiencing. The nobility, the chiefs and the leaders of the conservative society were suspicious of the changes that were being proposed and gradually implemented. So, faced with what they considered an archaic order requiring urgent transformations in order for it to survive the colossal challenges of the day, they searched diligently for methods and models that they might emulate. It is interesting to note here that one of the major 'modern' innovations in Ethiopia, Ethiopia's admittance to the League of Nations and commitment to the principle of collective security, would become Ethiopia's main strategy of defense against foreign aggression. This was an abandonment of the traditional suspicion with which Ethiopia rulers had traditionally treated foreign notions and agreements, a decision that would have tragic consequences with the invasion and occupation of Ethiopia by Fascist Italy.

Another important factor was the introduction of new ideas of social and political arrangements. It can be said that the seeds of democratic thinking were introduced through the new parliament, in itself a dramatic development for the traditional society. Ethiopians were exposed to new ways of thinking about themselves and the socio-political order that governed their lives. One important result was the increasing recognition of a national character over regional identities, further eroding the divisive provincialism that had been promoted during the *Zemene Mesafint*, another blow for the hereditary nobility.

Despite its far reaching repercussions, it is surprising how little opposition the new Constitution evoked from the hereditary nobility, testimony of the extent to which Emperor Haile Selassie had succeeded in curtailing their power. One major exception was Ras Hailu of Gojam who refused to honor the summons to Addis Ababa in 1931 and was absent from the signing of the constitution and the inauguration of parliament. Among his major objections were the clauses reserving the throne to the progeny of Emperor Haile Selassie. Ras Hailu was himself of royal descent making him a potential contender to the throne. The constitution terminated that eligibility. Additionally, the sweeping reforms that wiped away the autonomy with which he was accustomed to ruling Gojam were unpalatable to him.

In 1932, Addis Ababa was rife with rumors that Ras Hailu was organizing a plot against the new emperor. Characteristically, Emperor Haile Selassie bided his time until the opportunity to effectively entrap his contender presented itself. The plot against the emperor hinged on securing the release of Lij Iyassu from his incarceration in a house at Fiche, a town on the road between Addis Ababa and Debre Markos, the capital of Gojam. Lij Iyassu had been entrusted to the care of Ras Kassa, a religious and mild mannered personality. The conspirators believed Ras Kassa might be convinced to allow Lij Iyassu to throw a banquet where he would use the occasion to distract his guard and escape.

As much more information regarding the conspiracy reached the palace, Ras Kassa, entirely loyal to Emperor Haile Selassie, was asked to write a letter to Ras Hailu indicating his support for subversive action. It was decided that based on the response that Ras Hailu gave to this overture, measures would be taken against him. Ras Hailu fell for the ruse, responding to Ras Kassa's letter with expressions of his own treasonous intentions. Arrangements were then made for Ras Kassa and Ras Hailu to meet, but instead of Ras Kassa the emperor sent his army to rendezvous with Ras Hailu, at which point he was promptly arrested and brought back to Addis Ababa. Tried and found guilty of treason, he was fined 300,000 Maria Theresa thalers, his lands and properties were confiscated, and his governorship of Gojam granted to Ras Imru, the lifelong friend and trusted confidant of the emperor *(Mosley, 181)*. The death sentence for treason was commuted to life imprisonment – a decision interpreted by some as an act of benevolence – but also a decision made according to laws prohibiting the capital punishment for persons of royal lineage.

In the meantime, Lij Iyassu went along with his planned escape, leaving the banquet disguised as a woman *(Mosley, 182)*. He had heard about the arrest of his co-conspirator, but was convinced that if he made it to Gojam he would be safe from the emperor's soldiers and would be able to organize a force against him. However, a powerful rainstorm having rendered travel virtually impossible, he was caught and put in gold chains, an honor reserved for prisoners of noble birth. This time Lij Iyassu was banished to a rural prison house in Harar, where he would stay in isolation until his death in 1935.

The other major event of this period in terms of eliminating regional powers came with the subjugation of the semi-autonomous region of Jimma ruled by Abba Jiffar II. Emperor Menelik had granted the region semi-autonomous status in return for peaceful assimilation into the empire *(Bahru, 144)*. Following this agreement with Emperor Menelik, Abba Jiffar even assisted the emperor in his efforts to subdue other rebellious groups. Under Emperor Haile Selassie Jimma, like Gojam, lost its semi-autonomous status and became a province integrated into the new Ethiopian structure.

Parallel to the consolidation of power and the process of empowering the center at the expense of the regional chiefs, Emperor Haile Selassie continued on the path of realizing his personal vision of modernizing Ethiopia. Military projects that had begun prior to the coronation continued. With Belgian support an efficient, well-trained and well-armed Imperial Guard was established in the 1930's. With Swedish assistance the first professional military training academy was set up at Holetta, west of the capital.

On the education front, more Ethiopians were sent abroad to receive their education, while members of the emerging educated class became important figures in the evolving government structure and bureaucracy. New forms of governance were experimented with and the changes taking place throughout the country were such that the emperor could continue to claim to be an anti-feudal reformer.

With regard to foreign affairs, the overriding concern of Emperor Haile Selassie was the safeguarding of Ethiopia's independence. In his bold efforts to maintain this sovereignty he followed a radically different path to his predecessors. While Emperor Menelik had joined such international bodies as the Universal Postal Union and had signed the Treaty of Brussels regulating the international arms trade, his policies were nonetheless heavily influenced by the xenophobic Empress Taitu. Emperor Haile Selassie was much more single-minded in his approach and embraced the high-minded, though soon to be proven hollow, concept of collective security upon which the League of Nations had been established.

While Emperor Haile Selassie was pushing forward with his modernization agenda, the situation in Europe was beginning to turn. In 1923 Italy had been one of Ethiopia's key supporters in her successful bid to join the League of Nations. The following year Ras Teferi and his entourage had received a tremendous welcome in Rome. Over the course of the decade Italy had even offered to cede the port of Assab to Ethiopia *(Bahru, 151)*. In 1928 Ethiopia signed a treaty of friendship with Italy, and in 1930 the Italian Royal family sent a representative to Haile Selassie's coronation.

As the 1930s progressed, this friendly relationship between the two governments would undergo drastic changes. Fascism, which was firmly in place in Italy, in due course led to the resurgence of imperial ambitions and the determination to avenge the unforgotten humiliation by Ethiopia at Adwa.

The advent of Adolf Hitler and Nazism in Germany with a concomitant rise in militarism and bellicose posturing, resulted in a nervous Europe. Both France and Britain looked upon an alliance with Italy as a counterweight to the rapidly growing strength of Germany.

To the great misfortune of Ethiopia the chess-like manoeuverings of the European powers were played out in the Horn of Africa. Beginning with the Tripartite Treaty of 1906 Britain, France and Italy had exchanged secret agreements defining their respective spheres of interest in Ethiopia in defiance of Ethiopian sovereignty. In 1925, in the face of Ethiopian attempts to break away from dependence on Britain, France, and Italy for its development efforts, Britain and Italy signed an accord whereby Italy would support Britain's own ambition to build the Tana Dam. In return, Britain would endorse Italy's right to construct a railroad connecting Italian Somaliland with Eritrea through Ethiopian territory, as well as granting Italy exclusive economic rights over western Ethiopia *(Marcus, 74)*. The threat to Ethiopian sovereignty was diffused by a very strong protest by Ras Teferi at the League of Nations, a vociferous propaganda campaign against the two colonial powers by the Young Ethiopians, and with French diplomatic support *(Marcus, 77)*. At that juncture, Ethiopian membership in the world body was successful in upholding the sovereign rights of the country. This, however, would not always be the case.

In December 1934, the Wal Wal border incident occurred. Italian forces from Italian Somaliland clashed in Ethiopian territory with Ethiopian troops accompanying a group of officials, who were in the area to demarcate the border. This led to protest at the League of Nations, and an official inquiry cleared both Italy and Ethiopia of blame for the clash. Italy was exonerated in part because Italian forces had been in occupation of the areas in question since 1928 without Ethiopia protesting. The fact that, regardless of the timing of occupation, Italy was on Ethiopian territory was a fact completely ignored by the League of Nations Commission. Instead discussion focused on determining who fired the first shot, leading to an admonition of Ethiopia for having a significant military presence in the area, a situation which the Commission supposed could have been interpreted as a sign of hostile intent *(Marcus, 164)*. Italy demanded reparations from Ethiopia for losses suffered as a result of the incident, stubbornly proclaiming total innocence in the matter.

Under the pretext of the Wal Wal incident, used as evidence of hostile Ethiopian intentions, Italy speeded up the mobilization of troops in preparation for the invasion of Ethiopia. At this point both the French and British, completely abandoning the principles of the League of Nations, provided Italy with tacit approval of her designs on Ethiopia, providing the go ahead for subsequent Italian aggression. By January 1935, French Premier Pierre Laval and Mussolini had entered into secret agreements whereby France would abandon Ethiopian interests in return for alliance with Italy as a check against German aggression. The British went along with French policy. In a report prepared by a committee chaired by Sir John Maffey, permanent undersecretary of the Colonial Office, it was declared that there were no vital Britain interests at stake in the event of an Italian invasion of Ethiopia *(Marcus, 163)*. Italy took this as a green light for invasion.

Beginning with the Wal Wal incident Ethiopia had lodged protest against Italy at the League of Nations. Despite calls for the cessation of all hostilities, the Italian military build-up continued. In May 1935 Britain, France and other arms producing nations instituted a ban on weapons sales to both Italy and Ethiopia. The ban had a disproportionate effect on Ethiopia, who was totally dependent on imports, whereas Italy had the means to produce arms. While feeble attempts to bring about conciliation proceeded, the Italian build-up continued. Finally, on 3 October 1935, the Italians crossed the Mereb River without a declaration of war and the invasion of Ethiopia began.

The League introduced sanctions against Italy, but they were to have little or no effect on the situation. Sanctions against Italy proved ineffective as they covered arms and products that were manufactured in Italy itself. Neither did the British, who controlled the critical Suez Canal through which Italian weapons and troops had to pass, move to block this vital transportation link. However, with regard to Ethiopia, the Anglo-French embargo was severely debilitating.

France and Britain, in complicity with the Italian occupation, and in blatant violation of the League of Nations' principles, recognized the victories of Italy in Ethiopia. Under the

Hoare-Laval Plan, named after the foreign minister of Great Britain and the premier of France, it was proposed, as a way of bringing about peace, that Italy would acquire Ethiopian territories in the Ogaden and parts of Tigray as an area of economic influence. These absurd suggestions would lead to scandal in their respective capitals, forcing both politicians to submit their resignations *(Bahru, 166)*.

By the time Ethiopia began mobilizing troops, it was too late to mount an effective campaign. The Italians had taken every measure to ensure that the experience of Adwa would not be repeated. The assembled Italian force was numerically and technologically superior to anything Ethiopia could muster. The Italians were equipped with a significant air force and an arsenal that included the banned chemical weapon mustard gas. They would use these weapons to devastating effect, breaking Ethiopian resistance and allowing them to make rapid advances into Ethiopia. Almost immediately into their campaign the Italians found willing collaborators in Ethiopia, particularly among nobles and peoples negatively affected by Emperor Haile Selassie's reforms, including the emperor's own son-in-law. Dejazmach Haile Selassie Gugsa, son of Ras Gugsa Araya who had been the governor of eastern Tigray. He had been married to Princess Zenebe Worq, Emperor Haile Selassie's second daughter, in a strategic alliance linking the Emperor's family with the noble houses of Tigray. The princess died of influenza on 25 March 1933. Upon the death of Ras Gugsa a month later, the emperor declared Ras Seyoum, the grandson of Emperor Yohannes IV, governor of the whole province of Tigray, with Dejazmach Haile Selassie in practical terms retaining nominal control of eastern Tigray under him. The forced submission to Ras Seyoum distressed the emperor's son-in-law and he immediately made overtures to Italian officials based in Asmara. When war broke out, Dejazmach Haile Selassie was among the first to betray the Ethiopian cause *(Marcus, 140)*.

Emperor Haile Selassie had declared previously that in the case of war he would be the first in line to fight against the enemy. On 28 November 1935 he traveled to the town of Dessie in Wollo where, together with the Crown Prince, the governor of Wollo and his favorite son Prince Mekonnen, the Duke of Harar, he set up his war headquarters. Italian airplanes bombed Dessie on 6 December and during the raid the emperor took part in the attempts to bring the planes down. On 20 December the Ethiopian army made its first moves in the north, near the town of Mekele. The engagement did not result in significant gains either way. However on 22-23 December the Italians used poison gas to turn back Ethiopian troops *(Marcus, 172)*. This was an ominous sign of things to come. Gas was subsequently used on the southern fronts to break the Ethiopian forces with much success.

In January and February of 1936, the Italians continued to attack the supply lines to Dessie. The Italian air force with its indiscriminate use of poison gas was able to severely weaken the Ethiopian forces. Steadily, the Ethiopian armies on the various fronts fell before the Italians. The final Ethiopian attack came in late March but was compromised by advance knowledge of the attack by the Italians. The ferocious Battle of Maichew lasted until 3 April, when the Ethiopian army went into full retreat. The next morning the Italian air force unleashed a full day of bombing and poison gas, a tactic which effectively broke the otherwise organized Ethiopian army *(Marcus, 178)*.

As Emperor Haile Selassie's army suffered increasing losses, morale and discipline broke down. His retreat to Addis Ababa after the devastating battle of Maichew demonstrated a collapse of order and his power in Ethiopia. The Azebu people in particular, paid off by the Italians and themselves responding with historical indifference and enmity to Emperor Haile Selassie, attacked the retreating army. Eyewitness reports indicate much carnage, with the route back to Addis Ababa strewn with dead and decomposing bodies *(Mosley, 226)*. On his way back to the capital, the emperor stopped in Lalibela for prayer and to celebrate Easter mass; a moment for quiet reflection on the great tragedy that was unfolding for his country, despite his most valiant efforts.

On 2 May 1936, Emperor Haile Selassie boarded a special train to Djibouti for a life of exile. For three days there was burning and looting in Addis Ababa as the remnants of the army raided the Palace and attacked the merchant shops of Arada, the main shopping district of the city. It was into this general state of chaos and anarchy that the Italian occupiers stepped in on 5 May, the 'civilizing' forces had arrived to restore order.

The Italian Occupation marked one of the darkest hours in Ethiopian history, certainly the darkest in the long reign of Emperor Haile Selassie I. Though the occupation never blossomed into full colonization and only lasted for a short period of time, for the first time in history Ethiopia was occupied by a foreign power. Yet much of the country remained free, and an extensive resistance movement never allowed the Italians rest. Ethiopians, including the famous Black Lion group made up of Young Ethiopian intellectuals, continued to fight throughout the entire occupation period. This incomplete 'conquest' was obvious to the international community, and several nations, including the United States and the USSR, never recognized Italy's claims.

The emperor's choice of action throughout this period, including his decision to leave for exile during the nation's greatest hour of need, raises questions regarding the wisdom with which he handled the crisis. The emperor had in effect put the fate of Ethiopia in the hands of the League of Nations. As the leader of a sovereign state it was well within his mandate and it should have been his duty to respond with his own military preparation to the evident massing of Italian troops and weapons in Eritrea and Somaliland. Emperor Haile Selassie instead chose to respond diplomatically through protests at the League of Nations, a path that precluded a military response on his part. No preparations for war were made prior to the Italian invasion, and only in 1935 did the emperor begin ordering significant levels of arms, which following the declaration of an arms embargo against Ethiopia and Italy would remain undelivered in Djibouti. Prior to the invasion, Ethiopia had also withdrawn forces from the frontier to demonstrate Ethiopian commitment to the principles of the League and to avoid Italian charges that Ethiopia had started the war. These decisions proved grave miscalculations by a leader who had previously displayed such sharp political acumen. In retrospect it is baffling that Emperor Haile Selassie could have placed so much faith in the League, especially considering Ethiopia's history of continuous betrayal by foreign powers.

While many have been quick to criticize the emperor's decision to leave for exile, the harsh reality is that had he stayed on to fight he would either have been killed or captured. Thanks to his timely departure he was able to present and plead Ethiopia's case before the world. Had he been captured or killed it would have been easier for the Italians to install a puppet emperor and force the submission of the populace. When the decision was made for the emperor to leave Ethiopia none of the Council expected that it would be for five years. It was expected that after presenting Ethiopia's case before the League of Nations he would return to lead the fight from the temporary capital at Gore.

During the occupation the emperor was in regular contact with the Resistance, and his continued survival remained a source of inspiration, courage, and hope for them. Ultimately, following Italy's entrance into the world war on the side of Germany, the emperor's presence in Britain allowed him to take advantage of the sudden reversal in alliances and position himself to return home accompanied by a British fighting force capable of dislodging the Fascists. When Ethiopia was finally liberated in 1941, it was his presence and unique political skills that ensured that British plans to either dismember Ethiopia or turn her into a protectorate were frustrated. Had he stayed on to fight and die heroically, he would have been unable to save Ethiopia.

Ethiopia proved the ultimate test of the League of Nations' commitment to the founding principle of collective security. The League failed miserably. Individual state interests proved much stronger than considerations of collective security. The principle of collective security was never invoked on behalf of Ethiopia and following his address to the League on 30 June 1936, Emperor Haile Selassie made his famous prophetic statement, "it is us today, it will be you tomorrow."

LATE 1930S PROBABLY BATH

THE ROYAL FAMILY IN EXILE IN ENGLAND

from left to right: STANDING PRINCE MEKONNEN, THE CROWN PRINCE, EMPRESS MENEN,

H.I.M., PRINCESS TSEHAI, PRINCESS TENAGNE WORQ

sitting: PRINCESS HIRUT DESTA, AMHA DESTA, PRINCE SAHLE SELASSIE, PRINCESS AIDA DESTA,

ESKINDER DESTA, PRINCESS SOPHIE DESTA

THE CONQUERING LION OF THE TRIBE OF JUDAH PREVAILS

EXILE IN GREAT BRITAIN MARKS THE NADIR IN THE LIFE OF EMPEROR HAILE SELASSIE. THE EMPEROR, HIS FAMILY, AND ENTOURAGE SAILED FROM THE PORT OF DJIBOUTI TO JERUSALEM WHERE THE ETHIOPIAN ORTHODOX CHURCH MAINTAINS A CHAPEL AND SMALL COMMUNITY. AS A FORETASTE OF HIS NEW DIMINISHED STATUS EMPEROR HAILE SELASSIE WAS NOT MET BY HIGH OFFICIALS AS BEFITTED HIS RANK, NOR WAS HE WELCOMED TO JERUSALEM AS HAD BEEN EXPECTED AS THE OFFICIAL GUEST OF THE BRITISH HIGH COMMISSIONER *(Mockler, 146)*. INSTEAD, HE STAYED AT THE KING DAVID HOTEL AND MADE PLANS FOR SUBSEQUENT MOVES.

On 10 May, the emperor sent a telegram to the League of Nations reminding the member governments of their responsibility to uphold the principles of the charter, as well as their failure to deliver on promises they had made. In Great Britain, the public sympathized with the emperor's plight and the British Government felt obliged to offer refuge.

Arrangements were made for the emperor and some of his entourage to travel to Britain. On 23 May 1936 they sailed from the port of Haifa aboard a British Navy ship, sent by Prime Minister Baldwin to ensure the emperor's safe passage through the Mediterranean. As soon as potential danger from Italian naval attack had passed, however, the military escort, which was deemed too high a profile and too official for the exiled emperor was ordered to make a stopover in Gibraltar. Prime Minister Baldwin did not want it to seem that by arriving on a Royal Navy ship the emperor was an official guest of the British Government. Under the pretext that the military ship was unfit to continue the voyage, the group was moved to a civilian vessel headed for the port of Southampton *(Mosley, 239)*. The emperor arrived in

London on 3 June to a warm welcome by the British people who, unlike their vacillating government, had not abandoned the favor with which they viewed him *(Mockler, 150).*

The official reception of Emperor Haile Selassie in London was far from friendly. Indications of British officialdom's disdain for the Emperor had started with the British High Commissioner in Palestine creating pretexts for not meeting him officially in Jerusalem *(Mosley, 237).* A major reason why the emperor was entering a life of exile in Great Britain was because of British policy in favor of Italy and at the expense of agreements made with Ethiopia and the League of Nations. His presence in Britain was therefore a reminder of the British Government's duplicity and a source of some embarrassment. King Edward VIII refused to receive him and Prime Minister Baldwin resorted to hiding behind a table to avoid meeting him when he lunched at the House of Commons *(Mockler, 151).* With Ethiopia defeated, and the Italians in control of Addis Ababa, British politicians were even calling for the lifting of sanctions against Italy on the grounds that they no longer served any purpose.

On 30 June 1936, Emperor Haile Selassie stood before the League of Nations and, following the expulsion of members of the Italian media who had reverted to booing and catcalls when the emperor took the podium, made his historic and prophetic appeal on behalf of his country, occupied Ethiopia.

Following his unsuccessful appeal, Emperor Haile Selassie returned to a life in exile in Bath, England. Emperor Haile Selassie had come to Great Britain accompanied by three of his children, the rest of the family staying in Jerusalem with the Empress Menen. In September 1936 the empress, accompanied by Princess Tsehai and Prince Sahle Selassie, joined her husband at the villa named Fairfield he had purchased in Bath. The emperor had left Ethiopia with insufficient funds to maintain the lifestyle he and his dependants had been accustomed to in Ethiopia. Ethiopian funds in the Bank of England had been frozen, and they were forced to sell off the few items of value they had brought with them, including the imperial silver plate with which Fairfield was purchased.

The Emperor and his family were first treated as a novelty, generating so much curiosity that trips were organized from London for spectators eager to view them *(Mosley, 242)*. The excitement gradually subsided, and the family settled down to life in exile. The emperor had not expected that his time outside Ethiopia would last long and had therefore not taken much in the way of resources. By the winter of 1937/38 the imperial family was seriously hard up, unable to afford more than one coal fire per day. A small group of hard-core Ethiophiles had taken up the cause of Ethiopia and the exiled emperor. They made sure that the plight of the Ethiopian people and the emperor-in-exile was publicized around the world resulting in an outpouring of public sympathy and support. Movements in support of Ethiopia emerged, particularly among peoples of African descent in the diaspora, and hundreds of African Americans volunteered their services to fight for the freedom of Ethiopia, now under Italian occupation.

A fund was set up in Britain in support of Ethiopian refugees of the war, an action, which would greatly ease the financial burdens on the emperor. The emperor was not only responsible for his immediate household, but was also supporting many of his fellow countrymen who had followed him into a life of exile.

In December of 1937, arrangements were made for Emperor Haile Selassie to thank his many supporters worldwide in a radio broadcast. On his way to the BBC offices in London the taxi he was traveling in crashed. Although he had been seriously injured and his collarbone was fractured he continued with the program without complaining or once indicating the tremendous physical suffering he was enduring. After the broadcast he attended a Christmas party at the Great Ormond Street Hospital, where Princess Tsehai was working as a nurse, and did not acknowledge his pain until he was back in Bath *(Mosley, 244)*.

Empress Menen had not taken to Britain well, with the terrible weather and the economic hardships putting a severe strain on her health. It got to the point where it was feared that she might pass away if she remained in England and so arrangements were made for her to travel back to Palestine. She was to stay at the Ethiopian chapel in Jerusalem with Prince Sahle Selassie *(Mosley, 244)*.

Life in exile continued to be difficult for the emperor. His health continued to suffer and in 1938 when he returned to the League of Nations to plead Ethiopia's case, he was unable to deliver his own speech but instead had to have it read for him. There was even speculation that he himself might not survive long, a cause for celebration among the Italians as his death would certainly help in breaking the resistance they were experiencing in Ethiopia. Until 10 June 1940, when Italy entered the Second World War on the side of Germany, a move which made Emperor Haile Selassie's resigned hosts his sudden allies, the atmosphere in Bath remained dark and despondent.

One important outcome of his time in exile, away from the hectic schedule of running an empire, was the start of his autobiography: *My Life and Ethiopia's Progress*. This remains an important document in understanding the life and times of the emperor, a valuable record for the study of modern Ethiopian history.

Meanwhile, back in Ethiopia, the Italian occupation of Ethiopia was never to be completed. Upon abandoning Addis Ababa in the face of the approaching Italian army, a provisional government of independent Ethiopia had been set up in the west of the country in the town of Gore. A certain amount of resistance was directed against the Italians from there, but by December of 1936 Ras Imru, who had been made regent and placed at the head of the Gore capital, was forced to surrender.

Resistance to Italian Occupation was evident from the very beginning. It would take a while before regular ambushes and attacks against Italians by Ethiopians hiding in the surrounding hills of Addis Ababa would stop. An attempt was made for a coordinated attack on the Italian occupied city by several groups of resisters. The brave attempt was destined to fail, but in the process Ethiopia got one of her first martyrs, Abuna Petros, who preferred to die rather than capitulate to the enemy. Following the defeat of the Italians the emperor ordered the erection of a statue in memory of Abuna Petros where it stands to the west of the municipality building in Addis Ababa, a reminder of the courage and bravery of the city's forefathers to this very day..

Although the fall of Gore marked the end of officially independent Ethiopia, resistance was a continuous characteristic of Ethiopia under the Italian Occupation. The mountainous and inaccessible interior of the country provided many pockets of territory that never fell under Italian rule, and the Fascists could never honestly claim to have fully pacified Ethiopia. Things came to a head on 19 February 1937 (Yekatit 12 according to the Ethiopian calendar) when the Viceroy Graziani held a public ceremony marked by the giving of alms to celebrate the birth of the Prince of Naples. In the midst of the festivities two Ethiopians of Eritrean descent, Abraha Deboch and Mogus Asgedom, lobbed several grenades into the group of gathered Fascist officials and other dignitaries. Graziani was injured in the attack, though not fatally. As he was rushed to the hospital, the Italian carabinieri began firing randomly at the gathered Ethiopians. Chaos ensued and in retaliation, Guido Cortese, the Italian Federal

Secretary, declared to the Blackshirts in Addis Ababa that Italian forces were allowed to kill and do what they pleased with Ethiopians for the next three days, as well as to burn and raze the city as they saw fit. The next three days were nightmarish as a general massacre ensued with helpless Ethiopians being gunned down, tortured, and put to death in the most horrific manner. Large parts of Addis Ababa burned. A particular group singled out for extermination were educated Ethiopians, members of the remaining intelligentsia who it was feared would instigate more plots against the occupiers. The larger part of a generation of Ethiopians, painstakingly educated in previous decades, was effectively wiped out.

As the Italians investigated the assassination attempt they discovered that one of the conspirators had traveled to the monastery of Debre Libanos prior to 19 February , and that monks from the monastery had come to Addis Ababa earlier that month requesting loans from the Administration. The perceived complicity of the monks resulted in instructions to exterminate the order. During the May celebrations of the day commemorating St. Tekle Haimanot, the founder of the Debre Libanos monastery, the wholesale slaughter of monks took place in retaliation for the attack on 19 February.

One unanticipated result of the Graziani and Debre Libanos massacres was to be the consolidation of national resistance against the Italians. In Gojam, for example, the Italians had first been greeted as liberators from the yoke of Emperor Haile Selassie's rule, particularly when it became clear that the former ruler of Gojam, Ras Hailu, had escaped from Emperor Haile Selassie and was an active collaborator with the Italians. However, Gojam was a bastion of the Orthodox faith, and news of the Debre Libanos massacre turned the Gojam people firmly against the Italians, and revolt broke out. The Italians reacted with a general movement against the Amhara, particularly the Shoan Amhara, who had put up the most resistance to their occupation and whose lands had remained completely outside the control of the Italians. Faced with the risk of annihilation, Ethiopians who had settled into an uneasy coexistence with the new rulers broke out in near complete rebellion against them. Important rebel leaders emerged to fan the flames of resistance, including such legendary names as Abebe Aregai, who repeatedly defied Italian attempts to capture him and became a living legend for Ethiopian fighters of the time, and Belai Zeleke.

While resistance continued to increase against the Italian occupiers, by 1939 members of the Ethiopian nobility, many of whom had been deported to Italy by Graziani but later released by his successor the duke of Aosta, as well as others who had capitulated, became an integral part of Italian local government and attempted to win over public support. The Italian leaders in Ethiopia took it upon themselves to appoint rases and extend titles, a prerogative that until their occupation was solely the domain of the emperor.

Emperor Haile Selassie had by this time an active group of anti-fascist supporters in Great Britain. A network had been established that kept him abreast of developments in Ethiopia. In 1939, true to his prophetic statements made in 1936, war broke out in Europe. With the entrance of Italy on the side of Germany, the tables turned dramatically for the exiled monarch. All of a sudden he became an ally of his host country, and his desire for assistance in fighting against the occupiers of his country was to be realized.

In Ethiopia, the absence of an emperor around whom patriots could rally had resulted in initial disarray and lack of cohesion among resistance groups. This would lead to searches for a possible replacement monarch. The children of Lij Iyassu emerged as potential candidates, and at one point an emperor was even declared (Meleke Tsehai Iyassu, crowned by the Patriot leader Abebe Aregai who was subsequently made Ras by the new emperor). The Italians were negotiating with some of the other children of Lij Iyassu hoping to find a new Ethiopian

Neguse Negest who would be an effective puppet in their hands *(Mockler, 190)*. All of this activity was reason for concern on the part of the emperor in exile, but there was never any real threat to his position as emperor. Meleke Tsehai Iyassu died soon after his 'coronation' and none of the other contenders was ever declared emperor. In fact, in the second volume of his autobiography the emperor reproduces a letter sent to him by Yohannes Iyassu declaring his loyalty to the emperor and describing his efforts in the struggle against the Italians.

In the second half of 1940, it finally became clear that a British-led invasion of Occupied Ethiopia was in the works. Four years after his departure from Ethiopia the emperor returned to East Africa, to the Anglo-Egyptian Condominium of Sudan. From the start it was apparent that a precise plan for retaking Ethiopia had yet to be devised and that adequate supplies and troops were not assembled. British officers in the Sudan were even reluctant to accommodate the emperor in Khartoum afraid of possible reaction from Italian forces to the east of the border *(Mockler,212)*.

Reclaiming his position as the proper person to head the Ethiopian forces that would accompany the British in their bid to take Ethiopia proved yet another challenge for the emperor. He ultimately persevered and after many false starts and months of simply waiting around the assembled force, named Gideon Force, began operations. In January 1940 Emperor Haile Selassie finally set foot on Ethiopian soil and raised the flag at the border crossing of Omedla. Seven months later, following fierce fighting and a campaign that would generate its own history of adventures and heroism, Emperor Haile Selassie re-entered Addis Ababa. The Conquering Lion of the Tribe of Judah had returned triumphantly. He had prevailed against nightmarish odds and obstacles and was finally back in his palace; ready to once again consolidate his hold on power and continue the mission he had embarked upon in the 1920s of modernizing Ethiopia.

Emperor Haile Selassie's return from exile allowed him to embark on a policy of reconciliation. He knew full well the evils perpetrated against his people by the Italian occupying force as he had been a personal witness to the horrors of chemical warfare.

When he returned to Ethiopia, the first victim of Fascist/Nazi aggression and the first to be freed, Emperor Haile Selassie told his people that there would be no retribution. He appreciated the potential contribution that skilled Italian labor could make to development efforts and declared that those Italians who chose to stay and live amongst Ethiopians were welcomed. It is important to keep in mind that there were instances of Italians of good faith and sound morality who defected to the side of right and fought alongside the Ethiopian patriots for the independence of Ethiopia.

In July of 1940, soon after the start of the Gideon Force campaign to liberate Ethiopia, Emperor Haile Selassie issued his Mercy Proclamation:

'By the Proclamation released on Hamle 17th, 1932, (24 July 1940) I announce to you that I advised the Italians in Ethiopia and who were completely encircled to submit to our Chiefs in order to avoid being killed. Consequently I recommend to you to receive in a suitable manner and to keep all the Italians who submit to you with or without arms. Do not reproach them for their atrocities to which they have subjected our population. Show them that you are soldiers possessing human feelings and a human heart. Do not forget that during the Battle of Adwa, the valiant Ethiopian warriors who had handed over the Italian prisoners to their Emperor have increased the honor and elevated the name of Ethiopia ...

... But We recommend to you to spare their lives and treat well the enemy which will represent humanity; We particularly recommend you to spare and respect the lives of children, women and old people. Do not pillage the goods of others, even the property of the enemy. We recommend to you not to burn any house.

'When I order you to respect all these things it is only to ask you to perform an act of conscience, because my heart tells me that the Ethiopian people is not unfair to any other civilized people in their respect for the laws of war.'

Later, upon his entry to Addis Ababa on 5 May 1941, in his victory day statement the Emperor recalled some of the tribulations that the nation had gone through, and again reminded his subjects not to seek revenge and retribution, for the occupation was over, the enemy was defeated, and the best possible outcome for the nation at that particular point was to treat the enemy with undue civility.

This is perhaps one of the most important legacies of Emperor Haile Selassie, and with regard to the Fascist adventure begs the question, who should have been civilizing whom? One can easily imagine scenarios where Ethiopians who had suffered at the hands of the occupiers chose to avenge their friends and family. Massacres of Italians could have been a logical consequence of the Ethiopian massacres. Had that happened, despite the fact that in the 1930s and 1940s it was Fascist Italian forces that were the perpetrators of crimes against humanity, the onus of world opinion would have most definitely turned against Ethiopia. Ethiopia's suffering would have been forgotten had there been retribution, and the villains would have in turn become the Ethiopians. It is important to acknowledge that it did not happen because of the leadership of Emperor Haile Selassie.

Another important part of this story of forgiveness is with regard to relations between the diverse cultural communities of the Ethiopian Empire. As part of their occupation tactics the

Italian forces had used the time tested methods of divide and rule implemented elsewhere on the continent by the British and other colonizers. The Italian scheme was simple; to set the southern peoples of Ethiopia against the Amhara and Tigray peoples of the north, whom the Italians identified as constituting the principal opposition to the complete pacification of the country. Ultimately the Italians were to realize the naiveté of their plans, finding that Ethiopian resistance to colonialism was not just a characteristic of central and northern Ethiopians but was true of the entire Ethiopian peoples. Some of the great heroes of the Ethiopian resistance were Oromo leaders, the patriotic Dejazmach Balcha who died in combat being one of the more celebrated examples. Though during the power struggles following the death of Emperor Menelik he stood in opposition to Ras Teferi, as soon as the call to arms to was sounded, he was one of the first to appear at the *Gibee* (the palace compound) announcing his loyal service on behalf of Ethiopia.

The principle of forgiveness extended beyond the former Italian enemy and included potential rivalries amongst Ethiopians themselves. It is a sad fact that there were traitors and collaborators who for personal gain and benefit accepted and embraced the occupiers' advances and worked to promote the colonial agenda to the detriment of their fellow Ethiopians. Bands of disgruntled or simply opportunistic groups were paid and encouraged to attack and raze villages where there was resistance and a common tactic employed was the strategy of castrating boys. The emperor's amnesty also covered these individuals and remains a fine example of his magnanimity. Otherwise ethnic tensions and clashes could have increased following liberation with various groups seeking revenge and demanding retribution for atrocities experienced during the occupation.

Territory Administration (OETA) however, made a sham of the terms 'independent' and 'sovereign'. The situation was a trying one.

The post-liberation period was the closest that the colonial powers got to achieving their vision of partitioning Ethiopia. With Ethiopia under the control of the OETA, the British colonial administration in East Africa intended to integrate the Ogaden with British and former Italian Somaliland to create what they termed Greater Somaliland. In the south, the Borana lands were to be integrated with the British colony of Kenya. In Eritrea, British designs were to integrate the lowlands inhabited primarily by nomadic Islamic communities with the British dominated Anglo-Egyptian Condominium of the Sudan. The rest of Eritrea would be unified with the Tigray region of Ethiopia and they would form an independent nation.

Ironically, these initial plans for the partitioning of Ethiopia followed the colonial administrative regions set up by the Italians and paid no attention to the fact that Ethiopia was an independent nation and an ally in the war that the British and Allies were waging against the Axis powers. British plans, in complete violation of Ethiopia's right under international law to maintain her pre-occupation lands, was a typical continuation of historic British duplicity in terms of relations with Ethiopia. Separating Tigray province and the former Italian colony of Eritrea from the rest of Ethiopia would have meant the complete dissolution of ancient Ethiopia as that region is where the foundations of modern-day Ethiopia lie. This is where the Axumite Empire flourished, and where the most important center for the Ethiopian Orthodox Faith, Axum's St. Mary of Zion is located. British plans for Ethiopia were a typical example of the broader African policy where new political units were created with complete disregard for the existing historical and cultural realities. Africa continues to suffer the consequences of these arbitrary divisions.

British intentions to carve up Ethiopia and to frustrate her hopes of reclaiming Eritrea, thereby regaining access to the sea, became a touchy situation for the emperor, one that would test all his diplomatic skills. On the one hand he owed a great deal to the British for hosting him in exile, and for facilitating his return to Ethiopia. However, the achievement would be entirely hollow if it meant the replacement of Italian occupation with him in exile for a British occupation with him as legitimizing puppet emperor in Addis Ababa.

From the beginning, the relationship between the emperor and the British administration was filled with tension and discord. In 1941, soon after his triumphant return to Addis Ababa, Haile Selassie appointed his first set of ministers to run his new government. This resulted in an angry response from the Occupied Enemy Territory Administration whose representative in Addis Ababa, Brigadier Maurice Lush, declared that "His Majesty cannot fully reassume his status and powers as Emperor until a peace treaty has been signed with Italy. Until that happens the King of Italy remains the legal ruler of Ethiopia." *(Mosley, 275).*

Naturally this was greeted with anger and indignation at the palace, and did not bode well for good relations between the British administration and the emperor. Although Ethiopia was a British ally contributing to the ongoing war effort against the Axis powers, the fact that Ethiopia's enemy was European inclined the British administration to be decidedly more sympathetic to the enemy than their ally.

Problems with the British presence extended beyond relations between the OETA and the palace. In the public arena the behavior of soldiers from the liberating forces proved an affront to Ethiopian sensibilities. Incidents between the liberating forces and Ethiopians, including confrontations with Ethiopian Patriots and members of the nobility, led to questions regarding Emperor Haile Selassie's status and the true nature of the British presence. Occasions where drunken South African troops threw Ethiopians out of bars seriously compromised the emperor's position amongst his own people. Ultimately, the emperor was forced to demand an agreement from London clarifying the relationship between Ethiopia and the British liberators. His communication resulted in a statement from Prime Minister Winston Churchill declaring British recognition of and commitment to Ethiopian independence and sovereignty. This silenced detractors at home, and ended OETA designs to carve up Ethiopia.

The First Anglo-Ethiopian Agreement was signed in January of 1942. Under the agreement the emperor was compelled to cede many of the prerogatives of a leader of a sovereign state to the British administration, including the right to declare war. British representatives were placed in a superior position over other diplomatic missions. Key advisory positions in the Ethiopian government administrative structure were likewise dominated by the British administration. In return, Ethiopia received limited and dwindling financial assistance from the British Government *(Spencer, 99)*. Perhaps the most sensitive concession forced upon the emperor was continued British military occupation of the Ogaden.

In 1944, the agreement was modified in favor of greater autonomy of action for Ethiopia and the emperor. British dominance over diplomatic representation in Addis Ababa, as well as their exclusive hold on advisory positions, was removed. The only significant concession that remained was British military occupation of the Ogaden.

Alongside the challenges to Ethiopian independence from the British administration, the emperor was faced with serious domestic challenges to his centralized rule. The continued presence and behavior of the liberating force created continuing ammunition for his detractors. In several parts of the country rebellions broke out. The Azebu or Woyane rebellion in Tigray, which was one of the most prominent, was eventually quelled with British military assistance.

The Italian occupation had damaged the fabric of Ethiopian society. The entire country had experienced economic and physical hardship. Populations were displaced, and in the aftermath of the war of liberation there were still roving groups of patriots and members of the local force set up by the Italian occupiers. Armed, and without adequate arrangements for their resettlement, many were surviving in the tradition of the Ethiopian *shifta* (bandits) living off the spoils of raids against travelers and settled peasant communities. The security situation required immediate attention. Among the first set of ministries set up was the Ministry of the Interior which, among other things, was responsible for improving the security situation in the country.

Among the first projects restarted by the emperor was the process of creating a modern military force for Ethiopia capable of defending her against any threat to her sovereignty. The recent experience of occupation, and the abysmal failure of collective security to guarantee that sovereignty, made this a critical priority. Parallel to this was the establishment of a modern police force capable of ensuring the security situation in Addis Ababa, as well as the other major urban areas in the country. The work of setting up the police force, as well as reestablishing a modern Ethiopian army, was begun with assistance from the British Military Mission to Ethiopia, resident in Addis Ababa.

The clashes between the emperor, with his desire and need to reclaim complete control of his country, and the British Administration under the Occupied Enemy Territory Administration, led to several decisions that have been interpreted as deliberate moves by the British to weaken and frustrate development efforts in Ethiopia in reaction to Ethiopian

1947 ADDIS ABABA

THE EMPEROR VISITING AN ELEMANTARY SCHOOL

defiance and determination not to be dominated. Among these clashes was the removal of Italian war booty from Ethiopian territory. As the victim of aggression that had resulted in tremendous losses for Ethiopia, maintaining whatever Italian machinery and other goods left over from the occupation effort would have been limited, though thoroughly justified compensation. The British ensured that this would not happen, instead shipping the various goods, including whole factories, to their territories in Kenya, British Somaliland and the Sudan. *(Pankhurst, 35-77)*. The captured Italian arms to use only one example, would have been a tremendous boon for the Ethiopian army.

Despite the many tragedies of the Italian Occupation, the brief period under European control had resulted in some important infrastructure developments for Ethiopia. The Italians had completed the basic network of paved roads emanating from Addis Ababa to the various administrative capitals in the regions.

In the aftermath of the attempt on the life of Graziani in 1937, the Italians had ensured the annihilation of virtually all the trained and educated Ethiopians who had remained in the country. Their absence was particularly felt once the reconstruction efforts of the post-liberation period began. In response to the amnesty and offer by the emperor to remain in Ethiopia and work, numerous skilled Italians opted to remain and work in the country. Throughout Ethiopia (not including Eritrea) there were approximately 70,000 Italians immediately after the liberation. The OETA, however, insisted on the repatriation of all Italians, forcing the roundup of many who had wished to stay on. These Italians, who had set up machine repair shops, and garages, and who possessed the technical skills for maintaining the infrastructural developments that had taken place, were considered important for the post-liberation development of Ethiopia, and this decision by the British was a disservice to Ethiopia. It is important to note that a significant Italian community did manage to stay on.

In spite of the violent beginnings to the relationship, the post-liberation period witnessed an important role for Italians in the development of the country, as well as surprisingly warm and friendly relations between Ethiopians and Italians in general.

As mentioned earlier, another immediate and major challenge for the emperor in the post-liberation period was maintaining the country's territorial integrity In this respect the emperor played the diplomatic field brilliantly, scoring major victories for Ethiopia. Upon liberation from Italian rule the former colony of Eritrea was initially placed under British control, as was the Ogaden, part of Ethiopia's Harar Region bordering British and former Italian Somaliland. To his credit Emperor Haile Selassie ensured that both these territories would revert to Ethiopian control.

In 1945, World War II came to a close with an Allied victory. During discussions regarding the fate of former Italian colonies the victorious Allies initially rejected Ethiopia's claim to Eritrea. The matter did not end there however, as a satisfactory solution could not be found as to the fate of the former colony. Within Eritrea there was overwhelming support for union with Ethiopia, although an Italian-backed independence faction also existed. This initial pro-Italian party later formed part of the independence bloc with the Muslim League. Britain, France, the Soviet Union, and the United States organized the first Commission of Inquiry to look into the Eritrean question, but were unable to come up with a solution. The Four Powers then forwarded the matter to the United Nations for further study. A second Commission of Inquiry, made up of Burma, Guatemala, Norway, Pakistan and South Africa was set up. The British were keen to maintain the Ogaden region and were willing to forego their designs for Eritrea to achieve this. Believing that Ethiopia was willing to make that concession they supported Ethiopia's bid for Eritrea at the United Nations. By the time they realized that the emperor would not budge on the Ogaden the majority of the UN was in favor of the Ethiopian position. Following a trip to Eritrea by the Commission in 1950 Guatemala and Pakistan favored independence, Norway recommended union, while South Africa and Burma suggested federation *(Bahru, 183)*. A compromise decision was finally reached to federate the former colony with Ethiopia.

With regard to the Ogaden, the emperor pressed on with his demands for complete British withdrawal from the area, particularly since the earlier justification for continued occupation, being in a war situation, was no longer valid. By 1955, the Ogaden region had been completely restored to Ethiopian control.

The many difficulties experienced by the emperor were further aggravated by a series of personal losses. In 1942, Princess Tsehai, the first Ethiopian nurse and an important reforming figure in the field of medicine, died due to complications caused by a miscarriage. In 1957, an automobile accident would take the life of the emperor's favorite son, Prince Mekonnen the Duke of Harar. Five years later in 1962 both Empress Menen and Prince Sahle Selassie passed away. Four of the emperor's six children died before him.

From the depths to which he had sunk with the Italian occupation and exile in Britain Emperor Haile Selassie rose to the pinnacle of his power and prestige in the 1950's. With the federation of Eritrea he achieved the centuries old Ethiopian ambition of regaining access to the sea. The federation was a formidable achievement with Ethiopian claims based on history, shared culture, language, religion, the need for access to the sea, and grounds of national security. Twice, assaults on Ethiopian sovereignty had been launched from Eritrea. Just as important, a significant proportion of the Eritrean population was now demanding unity with Ethiopia. A decade later the Eritrean Parliament voted itself out of existence and Eritrea became the fourteenth province of Ethiopia. That would trigger off rebel movements fighting for the independence of Eritrea, movements that would gain momentum following the emperor's downfall and would ultimately reverse the tremendous, hard-won victory of 1950.

In terms of the domestic political scene, many members of the hereditary nobility had died fighting during the Italian Occupation. Others that had capitulated to the Italians had in effect discredited themselves and were no longer threats to the emperor's power base. He assigned governorships of the various provinces to remaining members of the nobility and officials of state whom he trusted.

In 1955, for the twenty-fifth anniversary of his coronation, the emperor issued a revised constitution for Ethiopia, the major feature of which was the integration of the recently promulgated Eritrean constitution and elections. As with the previous constitution a major emphasis was regarding succession to the throne, again reserved exclusively for descendants of the emperor. The document established Ethiopia as a constitutional monarchy with a government of popular representation under two houses of parliament. In reality the constitution merely codified the supreme power of Emperor Haile Selassie, articulating his authority over all decisions and matters in Ethiopia.

The emperor's cabinet and ministers were largely made up of educated persons from humble origins, not from the hereditary nobility (although their influence on politics continued through the Crown Council, as well as their positions as governor of various provinces of the country). A large entourage of ministers and advisors surrounded the emperor, each group reporting to him the details of the every day happenings in the empire. The emperor had learnt well from the experience of the Menelik court, and used similar tactics of playing rivals against each other to receive information and maintain maximum control. The system would have its drawbacks, particularly towards the end of his career as the ministers and cabinet members became his exclusive eyes and ears on the empire and colluded in keeping vital information from him.

The immediate post-liberation period provided the emperor with the opportunity to achieve another objective that had frustrated previous rulers. The Abuna, head of the Ethiopian Orthodox Church, had up until that point, always been assigned from the Coptic Church in Alexandria. Historically this had given undue influence over Ethiopian affairs, always very much tied to the Church, to the Egyptian Coptic Church and by extension to the Egyptian State (and in later times to the British who occupied Egypt.) For example, the Abuna was the only person who could perform coronations of emperors or ordain bishops. The Abuna's power rested in his ability to excommunicate individuals from the faith, a powerful weapon that could be used in the politics of the country, as had been done against Lij Iyassu in 1916. For these reasons Emperor Haile Selassie, like his predecessors, felt the need to make the Ethiopian Church independent of Egypt. After careful negotiations with the Egyptian Coptic Church it was decided that Abuna Kyrillos who would be returning to Ethiopia following his departure during the Occupation, would be the last to be appointed from Alexandria. Since 1950 the Ethiopian Orthodox Church has operated as a completely independent church free from any influence by the Egyptian Coptic church.

Changes in the international scene in the post war period were to have a major impact on the emperor's program of modernization. One result of the Second World War was the significant loss of power and influence of the pre-war great powers, Great Britain and France. These two nations had played an important role in Ethiopian politics as colonial neighbors. World War II catapulted the United States to the position of super-power with dominance in the economic as well as military and political arenas. In stark opposition ideologically to the United States, the Soviet Union emerged as a military super-power carving out its own sphere of influence in the world. In the middle, between these two giants and the alliances that they fostered, emerged the non-aligned movement, in which Ethiopia under Emperor Haile Selassie as elder statesman would play an important role.

Despite the disastrous Ethiopian experience with the League of Nations, the emperor maintained his faith in the principle of collective security as a key means of ensuring global peace. In 1942, Ethiopia became one of the founding signatories to the Charter establishing the United Nations, and in 1945 was among the founding members present at the inauguration of the organization in San Francisco.

At the same time the relationship between Ethiopia and the United States took off with increasing US involvement in the emperor's development and modernization programs. In 1943, Emperor Haile Selassie sent a mission to the United States requesting military assistance, as well as financial and legal advisors. This initial approach resulted in the United States extending lend-lease assistance to Ethiopia, and the arrival of an American technical mission in Ethiopia in 1944. In the immediate post-liberation period the OETA had imposed the East African shilling as the working currency of Ethiopia. Ethiopian farmers, however, refused to accept the new currency insisting instead on being paid for their harvests in the traditional Maria Theresa thaler *(Spencer, 105)*. Ethiopian grain harvests were in high demand for export during the world war, and this drove up the price of Maria Theresa thalers, devaluing the East African shilling. By 1943 a solution had to be found. Securing the means for establishing an indigenous currency became an urgent task for Emperor Haile Selassie's new government. The 1943 mission was able to secure a significant loan from the United States for this purpose, a major step toward ending Ethiopian dependence on Great Britain *(Spencer, 106)*. These moves were significant assertions of Ethiopian independence, and signaled the emperor's determination not to become overly dependent on the British. In

1945, the emperor traveled to Egypt where he met with the American President Franklin Roosevelt. One of the outcomes of the meeting, perhaps in a move to detract from British claims over the Ogaden, was the granting to the American owned Sinclair Oil Company the rights to search for petroleum in the Ogaden region. Regardless of the existence of reserves, the move was an important expression of Ethiopia's claim to the region.

The rapid polarization of the post war international scene and the race between the two super powers to establish control over key geographic areas initially benefited Ethiopia. The communications center that had been set up by the Italians in Asmara, Radio Marina, became a major asset for the US military. Until the advent of satellite technology it would remain an important station in the US global communications network. Securing access to the communications base became a strategic reason for US support at the United Nations for the return of Eritrea to Ethiopia.

Another significant outcome of the new Ethiopia – US relationship was the establishment of Ethiopian Airlines. In 1945, the Ethiopian government signed an agreement with the American carrier Transcontinental and Western Airline (TWA) for setting up an Ethiopian airline. Ethiopian Airlines brought a new dimension to domestic travel, facilitating enhanced communication and the transport of people and goods across the country. The airline would grow to become the proud owner of the most extensive network across the African continent, providing critical links among African nations, and facilitating the increasingly important role that Ethiopia was playing in the diplomatic affairs of the continent. Ethiopian Airlines remains the pride of all Ethiopians.

The 1950s also presented Emperor Haile Selassie with an opportunity to demonstrate again Ethiopia's commitment to the principle of collective security. The advent of nuclear

JUNE 1958 OFFICIAL VISIT TO EGYPT

center from left to right: PATRIARCH JOSAB OF ALEXANDRIA, H.I.M.

IMPORTANT IMPROVEMENTS IN THE RELATIONSHIP BETWEEN THE ETHIOPIAN AND ALEXANDRIAN CHURCHES WERE ACHIEVED DURING THIS OFFICIAL VISIT TO EGYPT weapons and the ability of nations possessing them to inflict tremendous suffering and destruction with impunity rendered the world an even more dangerous place than in the 1930's. Following the outbreak of the Korean War and the United Nations decision to send a force in assistance to the invaded South, Ethiopia volunteered the services of a battalion from the Imperial Bodyguard *(Bahru, 186).* The emperor demonstrated to the world that even though the international community had abandoned their commitments to collective security in 1935-36, Ethiopia was a nation that honored its international obligations. Furthermore, it was a chance to display to the world that Ethiopia was now in possession of a modern fighting force capable of integrated action alongside the major armed forces of the world. The Ethiopian military was no longer the archaic traditional force that fell in the face of a modern European army a decade and a half earlier.

The Korean War came at a strategically important time for Ethiopia with a decision on the fate of Eritrea pending before the United Nations. Ethiopian participation in the United Nations force, as well as the commendable performance of the battalion, further inclined the world body in favor of Ethiopian claims.

Events in the Middle East in the 1950s resulted in Ethiopia becoming an even more important ally for the United States. In 1952, the Egyptian Revolution and the advent of the anti-American Gamal Abdel Nasser made Ethiopia, with her recently re-acquired Eritrean coastline, an important presence on the Red Sea. It was important for the US to maintain a presence along the narrow Red Sea corridor which was a vital shipping route for the supply of oil to the US as well as her allies in Europe and Japan. The establishment of the state of Israel following the close of World War II resulted in additional US interest in the region, as the US became the main ally and sponsor of Israeli security. Alliance with Ethiopia, the only non-Arab presence on the Red Sea Coast, was therefore of considerable strategic value.

In May of 1952, Ethiopia and the United States entered into an agreement that came to be known as the Point Four Program, which resulted in the signing of a treaty of friendship and cooperation the next year. The agreement covered cooperation in the areas of agriculture, public health, education, locust control, as well as public administration *(Bahru, 184)*.

In return for use of the communications base in Asmara, renamed Kagnew Station after the Ethiopian battalion that took part in the Korean War, the United States extended an extensive aid program to Ethiopia. This assistance was particularly important in the military and education sectors. Ethiopia soon became the highest recipient of US military aid on the continent, and over a two decade period 180,000 men had been trained and equipped, and a modern air force established *(Bahru, 186)*.

Emperor Haile Selassie had achieved another long-cherished desire of Ethiopian monarchs, the establishment of an effective fighting force trained in modern fighting techniques, equipped with modern weaponry, and capable of protecting and maintaining the territorial integrity and sovereignty of Ethiopia. The benefit of this modernization and training was tested in 1963 with the rapid repulsion of recently independent Somalia's attempt to occupy and take over the Ogaden region.

American assistance was to influence nearly all facets of development activities from the 1950s on. With assistance from the US, the Imperial Highway Authority was established which took over the task of road maintenance and development. Telecommunication facilities were placed under the administration of an Imperial Board. Although the expertise and equipment for the services was provided by the Swedes, the Americans influenced the administrative structure of the Board.

Modern education also took off in the post-liberation period with the urgent need to replace the educated class killed off by the Fascists, and the increasing need for educated and trained individuals to handle the requirements of the modernizing economy. Extra effort was made to include Eritrean youth in the educational program, as well as to provide them with employment opportunities upon graduation.

Emperor Haile Selassie's devotion to the spread of modern education was tremendous. With the re-establishment of the Ministry of Education soon after liberation, and the setting up of a National Education Board, of which the emperor was head, work began on opening primary and secondary schools throughout the country. New taxes were levied to support the new education system and rapid advances were achieved in the post-liberation period. All schools for Ethiopians had been closed by the Italians during the Occupation, so the emperor was starting literally from nothing. During the 1949-50 academic school year enrollment in primary schools had reached 49,077. By 1954-55, the number had increased to 79,000 *(Talbot, 185)*.

The opening of secondary schools also made significant progress. By the 1950s there were seven public secondary schools in Addis Ababa. Outside Addis Ababa, a Teacher Training School and Medhane Alem Secondary School were opened in Harar, Agricultural Secondary Schools were established in Ambo and Jimma, and a Public Health Center was set up in Gondar. Emperor Haile Selassie also opened the first secondary school in Asmara, and his name was bestowed on a private school opened near Massawa. Eritrean students no longer had to travel all the way to Addis Ababa to receive a secondary school education.

In 1950, Ethiopia's first college opened, the University College of Addis Ababa. By 1952 the Engineering College had been opened, and the Public Health College and Training Center opened in Gondar in 1954. The 1950s witnessed further expansion in the tertiary education system with the establishment of the Institute of Building Technology, College of Agricultural and Mechanical Arts, Harar; Marine Training Institute, Institute of Technology, and Military Training Institute *(Talbot, 195)*. The highpoint in the educational program came with the establishment of Haile Selassie I University in 1961, which was located on the grounds that used to house the emperor's palace, and which became an institution that embraced many of the colleges established previously.

Other important education and training institutions established by the emperor include the Technical School of Addis Ababa and the Commercial School, both of which became important sources of administrative and office personnel in all sectors of the economy. Training programs were also established under various ministries and departments. Vocational training centers, such as Her Majesty's Handicraft School, were also established. The Civil Aviation School, set up as part of the Ethiopianization program at Ethiopian Airlines, has evolved to become one of the highly reputed, premier training institutes in its field on the African continent.

The Addis Ababa Fine Arts School and the Yared Music School would produce a new pool of artistic talent adding to the vibrant social atmosphere that was developing in Addis Ababa. New theaters opened, television was introduced, and a cultural renaissance was underway.

While educational facilities within Ethiopia were catching up to world standards, Ethiopian students were sent abroad for higher studies – many ending up in Great Britain and North America. This exposure to foreign lands, especially at a time when students the world over were reacting with increasing radicalism to developments in world politics, was to have drastic ramifications in Ethiopia. The Ethiopian student movements in North America and

Europe were born, movements characterized by their impatient desire to see major changes at home. These associations would come to influence their counterparts at home and bring the left-wing radicalism of campus politics to Ethiopia.

With the advent of the American Peace Corps program in the 1960s, the youth education program in Ethiopia received an additional boost. (There are varying opinions regarding the ideological effect that these Peace Corps teachers had on their Ethiopian students. It has been suggested that the teachers, recent graduates from American universities, were themselves steeped in the radical politics of the American student movement, and that they played a major part in influencing Ethiopian students' radicalization.) American influence in education went beyond the high school level and was significant in the various colleges, as well as in the Haile Selassie I University, whose academic system was based on the American educational model. This ubiquitous American presence would later be pointed to as one example of American imperialist penetration in Ethiopia.

The post-liberation period marked one of the longest periods of peace Ethiopia had experienced in centuries. This condition of peace allowed for significant developments, as can be seen by the remarkable progress in the emperor's personally supervised education program. The much-needed breathing space from a preoccupation with both domestic power struggles or threats to sovereignty from outside, allowed for significant strides in the development of the country. Building on the foundations for industrialization and the beginnings of commercial agriculture left over from the Italian Occupation, several key industries developed in post-liberation Ethiopia. Ethiopia embarked on an attempt at import substitution industrialization. Under this program several large outfits emerged including the sugarcane plantations and factories at Wonji and Metehara under the Dutch HVA group, with minority Ethiopian ownership. Other agro-industrial initiatives included cotton plantations, the development of a textile industry, and expansion of the production of traditional export products including coffee, cattle and leather. Mining was another area of development, principally at the Adola gold mine, as well as a platinum mine in Wellega *(Bahru, 200)*. With an attractive investment package and a virtually untapped resource base Ethiopia looked set for dramatic growth.

In foreign relations also the emperor's performance was outstanding. Parallel to the weakening of the colonial powers a wave of vigorous independence movements emerged on the African continent. Ethiopia, as the only country to have successfully averted colonialism, became a guiding force for these new nations, so much so that the Ethiopian tricolor, green, gold, and red, became the colors of choice for flags of many of the newly independent nations on the continent.

At the United Nations, African diplomats sought their cues from Ethiopia. With the ascendance of Pan-Africanism as an important ideological force, the Ethiopian perspective became an influential force capable of mobilizing significant voting blocs at the United Nations. The emperor's prestige and the prominent role that he started to play in international diplomacy led to Addis Ababa being chosen for the site of the headquarters of the United Nations Economic Commission for Africa. The emperor played an active role in the discussions regarding Pan-Africanism, and was particularly influential in breaking the stalemate between the two blocs that emerged, one favoring the complete political and economic union of the continent, with the other opting for economic integration as a more realistic goal. In 1963, Ethiopia hosted the gathering of the heads of state and government of independent African states, which led to the signing of the Charter setting up the Organization of African Unity that same year. The fact that these two organizations, the OAU and the UNECA are headquartered in Addis Ababa has rendered the city the diplomatic capital of the continent.

The 1950s were the undoubted golden years for the emperor. He finally achieved realization of the modernizing agenda he had begun decades earlier as a provincial governor. His crowning achievements were the establishment of Haile Selassie I University, and the substantial international prestige that he and the country were attaining. Emperor Haile Selassie had succeeded in opening up Ethiopia to the world. However, despite all the accomplishments of the emperor, a lot remained to be done to remove the burdensome yoke of poverty and under-development. New ideas brought with them increasing desire for even more change. Signs were emerging that all was not well in Ethiopia. As subsequent events would demonstrate, the very institutions and social forces that the emperor so carefully produced and nurtured were to cause his tragic downfall.

1972 ADDIS ABABA

THE LAST NEGUSE NEGEST, 225TH MONARCH OF THE SOLOMONIC LINE

STATE PORTRAIT ON THE OCCASION OF THE EMPEROR'S 80TH BIRTHDAY

THE LAST NEGUSE NEGEST 225TH MONARCH OF THE SOLOMONIC LINE

THROUGHOUT HIS CAREER ONE OF THE ENDURING CHARACTERISTICS OF EMPEROR HAILE SELASSIE I WAS HIS TENDENCY TO BREAK WITH TRADITION AND FORGE NEW PATHS. IN THE 1920S HIS TRAVELS OUTSIDE ETHIOPIA HAD SHOCKED THE SENSIBILITIES OF THE ARISTOCRACY IN ADDIS ABABA. IT WAS THE FIRST TIME THAT A REGENT AND HEIR TO THE THRONE HAD DARED TO LEAVE THE COUNTRY.

In the post-liberation period, travel outside Ethiopia would become routine for the emperor. These trips to all corners of the world elevated his image as well as the international perception and understanding of Ethiopia.

It seems travel abroad became a more fulfilling activity for the emperor than dealing with the frustrations of domestic rule. As time passed, with criticism of his rule mounting at home and infighting increasing among his circle of advisors, the appreciation of foreign hosts and audiences must have been refreshing. Critics of his rule often cite these travels, claiming that he increasingly ignored domestic concerns. While it may be fair to criticize the emperor's handling of domestic affairs, under Emperor Haile Selassie Ethiopia attained an incredible international prestige, a far cry from the early decades of the twentieth century when he was just beginning his quest for power. In the 1960s this was evident on the African continent through the role the emperor played in the decolonization movements and his support for Pan-Africanism. Ethiopia under the emperor was a considerable force within the newly formed non-aligned movement and a respected voice at the United Nations, preaching on issues of international morality and justice. Emperor Haile Selassie was admired and respected throughout the world and through him Ethiopia and Ethiopians acquired respect.

The most serious challenge to Emperor Haile Selassie's rule came during one of these state visits abroad. In 1960, while touring in Brazil, word arrived that a coup d'etat was underway in Addis Ababa. The Imperial Bodyguard under the leadership of Brigadier General Mengistu Neway, in collaboration with his intellectual brother Girmame, had gathered the emperor's cabinet and ministers to the Guenete Leul Palace under the pretext that the empress was gravely ill. On 14 December 1960, citing dissatisfaction with the general backwardness of Ethiopia, they proclaimed to the nation that a new government was established with the Crown Prince as constitutional monarch and Ras Imru Haile Selassie appointed as head of the new government.

Although the rebels promised pay raises to all members of the armed forces, they had failed to secure the collaboration of the army and air force. This slip-up would ultimately result in their failure and demise.

Upon hearing of the coup d'etat the emperor cut short his visit to Brazil to handle the unexpected crisis at home. He flew to Asmara and coordinated the anti-coup measures. As the army and air force remained loyal to the emperor, within a matter of days the coup attempt had been aborted. To ensure that the army would have no material reason to consider siding with the rebels the emperor matched the rebel's promise for a pay raise for members of the armed forces. Additionally, the rebels had failed to generate much public support. Ethiopia still held the position and person of the emperor as the defining symbol of the whole country. The emperor was Ethiopia and the people were not yet open to the idea of rebelling against him and instigating a new order.

In the dramatic final moments of the coup attempt the gathered dignitaries in the palace were summarily shot. Girmame Neway died in the fighting that ensued. His brother Brigadier General Mengistu Neway escaped, only to be captured on the outskirts of Addis Ababa. He was subsequently tried and hanged.

Emperor Haile Selassie returned triumphantly and to a tumultuous public welcome. Having handled the whole crisis with his legendary calm, he was back and firmly in control. The Imperial Bodyguard, the elite force responsible for his security, was disbanded. The Crown Prince, who had apparently acceded to the rebels' demands under duress, was pardoned although he would never regain much favor with his father. After replacing those members of his cabinet who had died in the palace shooting, the emperor proceeded with his general program seemingly unfazed by the failed attempt to unseat him.

The Neway brothers were a microcosmic hint of the alliance of forces that would eventually succeed in bringing the emperor down. Within one family were represented two of the most prominent institutions created under the emperor's modernizing agenda; the Ethiopian intelligentsia, fruit of his education program, and the modern Ethiopian armed forces. The 1960 coup attempt was the first indication that, although the traditional threats to his power from the nobility had been virtually eliminated, the seeds of his undoing had been sown in the social forces he had personally unleashed. It is interesting to note that during the early decades of the twentieth century the nobility had been highly suspicious of the emperor's modernizing agenda, seeing the undoing of ancient traditions and customs. The 1960 coup attempt and the events of the next fifteen years would bear out their fears as ideologies completely alien to Ethiopia assumed ascendance and plunged the country into one of the bleakest periods of its history, destroying the ancient monarchy that had survived for three millennia without serious threat.

Although the 1960 coup attempt was unsuccessful, it had grave ramifications. From his days as regent the public relations machinery that the emperor had developed had created a sort of cult of personality around his person. His public demeanor including regular distribution of alms to the poor, traveling in convertible vehicles in full view of the crowds that lined the route of his motorcade endeared him to the common folk. If they ever felt that there was something wrong in the empire they never blamed him but instead his subordinates who were mere mortals and capable of making mistakes.

The many introductions to Ethiopia, the various 'firsts', such as Ethiopian Airlines, a university, modern schools, hospitals, theater, stadium, and television all occurred under the imperial brand. All was bestowed upon the people through his personal command and beneficence. Emperor Haile Selassie was the undoubted father of the Ethiopian people, not just any father but the Conquering Lion of the Tribe of Judah, the hereditary ruler on the Throne of Solomon, King of Kings, and elect of God.

The 1960 coup attempt created a hole in this bubble of omniscience. For a brief moment the emperor had been publicly held accountable for the economic problems of the country. More important, the idea that a military coup was a real option to unseat him and that Emperor Haile Selassie I was possibly fallible had entered the public psyche. The army for remaining faithful to the emperor was rewarded with the pay raise that it had been promised. This would be an important lesson, that loyalty need not be unconditional, that a price could be put on it and that with coordinated action it was possible to extract that price from government, the emperor himself.

The student body had by this point reached a sizable population and had also reacted to the coup attempt. Activists from among the student body had come out in public demonstrations in support of the coup leaders. Although there were no major demonstrations on the scale of what would take place in later years, the coup attempt was an indication of the possibility for mutually supportive action between the students and the military. In the Ethiopian context new socio-political forces had emerged. Although they were quickly contained in 1960, once the fuse was lit it would prove impossible to put out. New forces required new ways of dealing with them, a task that would prove too much for the aging monarch, despite his legendary skills.

In spite of this ominous sign of trouble within the empire, the emperor continued with his agenda full steam ahead. In 1960 he sent a battalion to join the United Nations Peacekeeping Force in the Congo. The emperor continued to push ahead with his international diplomacy, taking frequent trips abroad and playing host to many of the prominent monarchs and leaders of the world, entertaining them lavishly.

Emperor Haile Selassie continued with his firm support for the decolonization movement on the African continent. The cold war and the possibility of the total annihilation of mankind in a nuclear showdown provided fertile ground for lecturing on international morality and collective security. For the emperor the 1960 coup attempt quickly became an inconsequential event, the isolated work of a few disgruntled and ungrateful individuals.

Although the rebels in the 1960 coup attempt had not articulated it as such, one of the major underlying reasons for the continuing backwardness and the unsatisfactory level of economic development in Ethiopia was the land tenure system.

Trends in land allocation throughout the twentieth century tended towards increasing private ownership of land at the expense of the landless peasantry. In the post-liberation period, the allocation of land was used as a way of rewarding patriots, for settling exiles, and for rewarding demonstrations of loyalty. Absentee landlordism increased, and the situation of the peasant grew steadily worse.

Alongside these developments, changes in the tax system were also affecting the relationship between landlords and peasants to the detriment of the latter. By the 1960s while it was clear that changes were necessary, however each bill placed before Parliament that even hinted at land reform was soundly defeated by the landlord dominated institution.

The land issue became the principal cause adopted by the growing and increasingly radical student movement (other issues were also taken up, but none as forcefully as land reform). The student movement in Ethiopia was influenced from abroad where the sizable Ethiopian student population, organized into associations in Europe and North America, had in turn been influenced by the increasingly radical student movements around the world. That radicalism, with a penchant for demonstration and civic disobedience, and with a markedly left-wing ideological bent, infected the campuses of the University, the various colleges, and even the high schools in Ethiopia. Annual protests became routine with 'Land to the Tiller' as the defining cry (*Bahru, 195*).

The government did take some measures to quiet the protests. Leaders of the student groups were detained and expelled from school, subversive publications were forced to shut down. However, these moves were not enough to shut down the movement. More draconian measures could have been taken, and indeed there were those who advised the emperor to be stricter. Perhaps the emperor did not move more forcefully because the students demonstrating for reform were the same students that he had made personal visits to as they were growing up, going to their schools every week, or once a month, handing out sweaters, shoes, candies and other treats. Perhaps the emperor assumed that he would never be in personal danger and that the criticism, a lot of which he himself agreed with, was directed at his ministers and the parliament. They were a group that he was detached from and above.

In the late 1960s, commercial agricultural initiatives began to take off under a new government program promoting the sector *(Bahru, 194)*. One effect was to exacerbate the situation of the peasantry, as well as to create a new class of commercial farmers visibly benefiting from generous government programs, creating additional ammunition for radical Marxist style student protests. The situation with the peasantry would come to a head with the advent of the worst famine witnessed in twentieth century Ethiopia up until that point.

The year 1973 was disastrous for the emperor. On the foreign relations front Ethiopia would experience several setbacks that compromised Ethiopian security and the emperor's prestige. In the north, the Eritrean secession movement having acquired significant support from wealthy Arab nations was picking up pace. On Ethiopia's southeastern border, Somalia had recovered from her setbacks in the 1960s and with Soviet support was in possession of military capabilities exceeding those of Ethiopia. The Somali government had presented its irredentist claims before the UN Security Council. However, Ethiopia was successful in having the issue diverted to the OAU for decision whereupon it was decided that member states would honor the borders they inherited at independence. Although this was a move intended to maintain the stability of the continent by circumventing possible conflicts that would arise as a result of arbitrary borders, the decision was not accepted by Somalia which continued to develop its military. In response to the growing threats to Ethiopian security from the rebel movement in Eritrea and Soviet sponsorship of Somalia, Haile Selassie traveled to Washington DC to secure US support. The visit to the Nixon White House was a total disaster with the emperor leaving empty-handed. The emperor then traveled to

1950S TRAVELING IN ETHIOPIA

from left to right: CAPTAIN TADESSE, AIDE-DE-CAMP TO THE EMPEROR, H.I.M.

Moscow in an attempt to reduce Soviet military assistance to Somalia. The move was seen as an indication of weakness and Moscow instead insisted that the US close Kagnew Station in Eritrea. That same year the United States announced that it was closing its communications base in Eritrea marking the end of Ethiopia's strategic interest for the United States *(Spencer, 324)*. In a very short time the weakness of the Ethiopia relationship with the United States was revealed. By 1974, Ethiopia was virtually isolated in the world without meaningful allies and with plenty of enemies.

Domestically, 1973 was also disastrous for the emperor. The dependence of the majority of the population on subsistence farming for their livelihood, combined with vagaries of the weather, exposes Ethiopian peasants to the harsh reality of periodic famine. Famines are a regular occurrence in Ethiopian history and the twentieth century has had more than its fair share. Following two smaller famines in the post-liberation era, Tigray in 1958 and Wollo in 1966, the big one hit with a vengeance in 1973.

The world and much of Ethiopia discovered the 1973 famine through reports in the British newspaper the *Guardian* and a film prepared by journalist Jonathan Dimbleby. In October 1973, *The Unknown Famine* aired on television in Europe and the effect was remarkable. The extent of the human catastrophe unfolding was mind boggling, and so too was the apparent official Ethiopian policy to cover the whole thing up.

The Ethiopian public became aware of the ongoing famine in Wollo through friends and associates who had heard about the airing of the film on British television. The film resulted in a massive outpouring of aid for Ethiopian famine victims and in Addis Ababa there were unusual signs indicating a relief operation underway. Conflicting stories began appearing in the media, with simultaneous reports of drought and official denials of famine.

The famine of 1973 was the beginning of the end for the emperor's government. In January 1974, an army unit in Sidamo mutinied making a series of demands from the central government; the government, desiring a quick end to the matter granted their demands. In February the teachers went out on strike demanding pay raises for themselves as well as society-wide demands for a minimum wage and other reforms, demands which generated support for them from among other sectors of the public *(Teferra, 88)*. The teacher's protests were joined by student demonstrations.

The 1973 famine coincided with the global economic crisis precipitated by the OPEC oil price hikes, which had led to increases in retail rates at the gas pump. As though in perfectly calibrated coordination, taxi cab drivers also went on strike in February.

Again, the government did not react forcefully to the demonstrations – and it is important to note that public demonstrations were illegal at that time, meaning that the government could have acted more forcefully against the demonstrators. Instead, the emperor announced that gas prices would be adjusted, while telling the teachers that their issues would be resolved shortly. This response was not good enough for the teachers who maintained their strike. At the same time the rebellion in Sidamo had infected other branches of the military. Rebellion spread to Asmara; again the government acquiesced. Significantly, similar to the demands of the teachers, the armed forces demands were broad-based affecting all sectors of society. The government bowed to the demands of each military strike. The demonstrating soldiers would then return to their barracks proclaiming their loyalty to the government.

In February 1974, the continuing crisis compelled the cabinet to resign and a new prime minister was installed, Lij Endalkachew Mekonnen, and a new cabinet named. Still, the situation in the country remained volatile and the armed forces unpredictable. A committee was formed of the military and police to coordinate activity and restore order but to no avail. Public demonstrations and protests kept occurring. Ethiopian Airlines workers went on strike followed by Tobacco Monopoly workers, and laborers at other major industries and factories. As the public grew more accustomed to the power they were able to wield as a collective force, their demands began to change from pay increases to demands for public justice and for the dismissal of people who had abused their office; mass firings took place in several government departments. It seemed members of the lower echelons of every institution in the country, including priests of the Ethiopian Orthodox Church, were denouncing their superiors. And the protests kept on going.

Toward the middle of 1974 the military forces set up what was called a Coordinating Committee of the Armed Forces, Police and the Territorial Army, or Dergue, Ge'ez (and Amharic) for council *(Teferra, 121)*. A commission was also set up by the new cabinet to investigate accusations of corruption and abuse of office. The Dergue's guiding principles expressed in the declaration of *Ethiopia Tikdem* (Ethiopia First) became the guiding ideology. At the same time the calls for political reform were answered by the setting up of a body to review the constitution. These moves proved too little and too late, and the Dergue increasingly began to take action independently, arresting public officials throughout the country. In July, the Dergue forced the resignation of Prime Minister Lij Endalkachew Mekonnen, and the third prime minister to rule that year was put in office, Lij Michael Imru, son of Ras Imru, the emperor's cousin and childhood friend.

During 1974, Emperor Haile Selassie, who it is said had started going senile, ceased exerting any real power. As the year progressed the Dergue steadily took over all prerogatives of government and even arrested the emperor's daughter, Princess Tenagne Worq, and several of his grandchildren. The famine pervaded the general atmosphere of the protests through the year and was a central theme and justification whenever accusing government officials of wrongdoing. Initially the emperor was spared criticism, and in fact it is possible that the emperor was unaware of the famine and that his ministers and cabinet had deliberately kept the information from him. It was only after the BBC broadcast of the Dimbleby film that he was informed and in November 1973 he went to visit the Wollo camps *(Harrison/Palmer, 59)*.

As the Dergue continued to dominate the political scene, public accusations against the regime turned more and more to the person of the emperor. A campaign of vilification began and public protests against him mounted with the students leading calls for his abdication. The huge entourage that used to surround him gradually disappeared until, with his family either in prison or abroad, he was left alone with only his servants.

The emperor was accused of having stashed away millions, even billions, of dollars in foreign accounts. However, proof of these claims was never given. The public airing of such accusations severely diminished his image at home while the Dimbleby film had already tarnished his image in Europe. The vilification campaign culminated on Ethiopian New Year's Day, 11 September 1974.

Two years earlier, Emperor Haile Selassie had celebrated his eightieth birthday with great ceremony. On New Year's Day, Ethiopian Television (ETV) broadcast a film of that birthday celebration juxtaposed with images of the emperor feeding his pet dogs and extensive collection of animals, an aristocrat's wedding reception with a cake imported from London at egregious expense and Jonathan Dimbleby's film *(Harrison/Palmer, 61)*. The mass media, a vehicle so brilliantly utilized by the emperor, had in a short period of time completely destroyed his image. The following day Emperor Haile Selassie was deposed. In a move intended to further humiliate him he was led out of the luxury of his palace and driven to prison in the back of a Volkswagen Beetle. The man who used to ride in elegant motorcades waving to his subjects, who would invariably throw themselves to the ground in respectful prostration, was now on his way to prison in the back of a 'people's' car. There were no public prostrations that day, only the calling out of names including '*leba*' which means thief. It was a humiliating exit.

Details regarding his days as a prisoner of the Dergue are scanty. The emperor was apparently taken to the *Menelik Gibee* where he was imprisoned. The Dergue then offered the throne to the Crown Prince suggesting that he become constitutional monarch. Crown Prince Asfa Wossen, recovering in Switzerland from a stroke, never took up the offer. Finally in March 1975, the Dergue abolished the monarchy.

In June of 1975, Emperor Haile Selassie was admitted to hospital for an operation. Crowds of people came to visit him demonstrating his continuing popularity. However that was to be his last public appearance. Emperor Haile Selassie's tragic end apparently occurred on 27 August 1975, when the head of the Dergue, Colonel Mengistu Haile-Mariam, is said to have personally suffocated the emperor to death with a pillow. The following morning it was publicly announced that the emperor had died of a heart attack. The official statement declared that the emperor's doctor was unable to be reached, a statement that was most likely false as the emperor's doctor, the late Professor Asrat, was at home the whole time and could easily have been contacted either by telephone or messenger. He was not summoned to the emporor's bedside. Emperor Haile Selassie I, 225th ruler of the Solomonic Dynasty, died at the age of eighty-three.

1942 ADDIS ABABA

THE EMPEROR SITTING ALONE IN HIS CABINET

HIS ENDURING LEGACY

WITH THE DEPOSITION OF EMPEROR HAILE SELASSIE I ETHIOPIA ENTERED ONE OF THE DARKEST MOMENTS IN HER THREE THOUSAND YEAR HISTORY. IN A REMARKABLY SHORT PERIOD OF TIME THE SOCIAL, ECONOMIC AND POLITICAL STRUCTURES THAT HAD EXISTED FOR CENTURIES WERE COMPLETELY DISMANTLED AND A SYSTEM TOTALLY ALIEN TO ETHIOPIA'S DISTINCT HISTORICAL HERITAGE WAS INSTALLED IN ITS PLACE.

The revolutionary fire that had been lit by the students, workers, and the army blazed out of control, consuming the monarchy and landed nobility, while tearing through the fabric of the entire society. The Student Movement, instigator of the revolution in collaboration with the military, itself split into opposing camps. Once the main objective of removing the emperor was accomplished and the old system broken, the creation of a new order was next on the agenda.

Within the Dergue a ruthless campaign of eliminating potential threats to the emerging hegemony of Colonel Mengistu Haile-Mariam ensued. The Dergue quickly gained international notoriety for the scale and brutality of its repression. On 23 November 1975, the Dergue dismissed its chairman, Lieutenant-General Aman Michael Andom, on trumped-up charges. Four days later General Aman Andom was killed while resisting arrest. That same day fifty-seven former officials including one of the emperor's grandsons, two ex-prime ministers, as well as two Dergue members, were rounded up and executed on charges they were "attempting to disrupt the present Ethiopian popular movement" *(Teferra, 141)*. These first victims of the Dergue, popularly referred to as the 'sixty', have come to symbolize the tremendous waste of talent and devaluation of life that followed the end of the imperial system.

The Student Movement divided along lines favoring and in opposition to the emerging power structure within the Dergue. The student protests against the emperor and his government turned into bloody street battles, a period appropriately called the Red Terror.

From the start the ideological character of the revolutionary movement was left leaning. International events would push this tendency further so that by 1977 Ethiopia was no longer a non-aligned nation but firmly in the communist Soviet bloc. Somalia took advantage of this period of upheaval to launch an attack in pursuit of the Somali Government's irredentist policy that claims areas of Ethiopia that are populated by peoples of Somali ethnic identity as part of greater Somalia. The Eritrean separatist movement found this condition of Ethiopian weakness an opportune moment to mount renewed offensives. The movement gained in numbers and support as the atrocities being committed in the name of the revolution made independence an increasingly attractive option for the Eritrean people. The splintering of the revolutionary movement and the domination of a ruthless Dergue also resulted in the creation of new groupings opposed to it, including the Tigrayan People's Liberation Front that would lead the coalition of forces that would eventually topple the Dergue regime in 1991.

The Ethiopian student population, the military, the civil servants and the bureaucracy, the modern Ethiopians that Emperor Haile Selassie had personally created, turned on him in the ugliest manner. They betrayed the individual who had been like a father to them, who had cared for and fostered their very identity. These fomenters of the Revolution chose to ignore the fact that their ability to perceive that things required change and that they were in a position to propose alternative models, was a direct result of what the emperor had done. He had created a new social force in Ethiopia.

Just as these emergent forces in Ethiopian society betrayed the emperor, they too were in turn betrayed, by each other and by the new military regime. The student movement was ripped apart by ensuing events, as factions emerged fighting against each other, leaving the streets of Addis Ababa and other urban centers bloody and terrorized. From the high school level upward the youth of Ethiopia were consumed in the ferment. The campaign of '*magalet*', or exposing individuals opposed to the revolution, tore the fabric of society to shreds, as people turned on each other in attempts to save themselves. Some students became hard-line supporters of the new regime; the rest either fled into exile or else joined the various liberation movements that emerged to oppose the Dergue.

With both internal and external threats to the new government and to the territorial integrity of Ethiopia, the Dergue was in dire need of military assistance. Armaments ordered from the United States were held back in protest against the brutality of the regime as evidenced by the summary execution of the 'sixty' ministers and officers of the imperial government, as well as the nationalization policy of the Dergue. This forced the Dergue to search elsewhere for a military patron. The result was the remarkable reversal in cold war alignments of the Horn of Africa region as the Soviet Union, former sponsor of Somalia, switched alliances to fulfill the military requirements of the Dergue, while the United States, in counter measure, leaned toward support of Somalia.

With Soviet and Cuban military assistance, Ethiopia was able to reverse the Somali invasion. Soviet military support was used to temporarily quell the uprisings in the north and a protracted period of guerrilla activity ensued. In Addis Ababa and the major urban centers of the country the potential threat to the new regime from students was effectively removed with their dispatch to the countryside in the *Zemecha* (campaigns) designed to educate the peasantry and bring them out of illiteracy and poverty.

The Dergue's principal mechanism for substantiating its legitimacy and establishing a popular power base was by claiming to be looking out for the best interests of the masses, the peasantry and the emerging urban working class. This was a reflection of the popular revolutionary cries that had led to the emperor's downfall. The ruthlessness and terror that ensued was all justified in the name of the people. Land that was nationalized was justified in the name of the peasantry. The Dergue claimed to be giving land to the tiller in answer to the popular rallying cry that had brought it power, while in reality land became the sole property of the government, owned by neither the former nobility, nor the peasants.

A critical aspect of the Dergue's power consolidation process was to continue the campaign of defamation against the emperor and the order that he represented. The annual celebrations commemorating the emperor's downfall and the Revolution were invariably accompanied with proclamations denouncing the old order and television airings of the Jonathan Dimbleby footage alongside images of aristocratic excess. Throughout Ethiopia, anything symbolizing the old order was removed, including any statues and images of the emperor. Institutions that bore his name were all renamed. This reached the point where people were even afraid to mention the emperor other than to denounce him.

By the late 1970s, the Dergue was firmly in control of Ethiopia. The victory over Somalia added to its prestige and strength domestically. The rhetoric championing the poor of Ethiopia worked to create a broad constituent power base. Soviet and Cuban military assistance made opposition seem a futile exercise. Although the Eritrean separatist movement and other liberation forces continued their struggles against the government, it would take seventeen years before their combined efforts and the complete frustration of the Ethiopian people would lead to the downfall of the Dergue.

Nationalization and the economic policies pursued by the Dergue effectively halted the advances of the late 1960s and early 1970s. The moral bankruptcy of the new government was most glaringly exposed during the 1984-85 famine. As the Dergue spent millions of dollars on a tenth anniversary celebration, millions of Ethiopians faced starvation. Shipments of whisky intended for the celebrations were given precedence at Ethiopian ports over deliveries of much needed food assistance. The very scenario that the Student Movement and Dergue had condemned the emperor for repeated itself in greater measure a decade later.

Meanwhile, the exodus of Ethiopians into a life in exile continued unabated. Despite tremendous constraints placed on their ability to travel, hundreds of thousands departed for lives as refugees, ending up scattered all over the world.

The collective sense of being Ethiopian altered radically after the emperor's death. Prior to the revolution whenever Ethiopians went abroad for schooling, in almost every case they could not wait to return home to put into useful practice the new skills they had acquired. The 'brain drain' syndrome was inapplicable to Ethiopia, largely because of the emperor. This was due to the remarkable personal attention he gave to the educational program. The emperor was a regular visitor to schools, in Addis Ababa and throughout the country. He made regular gifts of books, candy and clothing, and was devoted to the well being of the students, continuously making personal checks on every detail of their lives. Among some of the many proclamations made following the emperor's return from exile in 1941 was the call to Ethiopian parents that stated: '*weldo yalastemare indegedele yikoteral*', or, roughly translated, 'parents who do not educate their children are effectively killing them'. Ethiopian society, in this regard, was completely transformed during his reign. From conservative and traditionalist reluctance to send children to modern schools, finding the means to educate their children became an essential part of parenting in Ethiopia.

1948–1949 GONDAR

THE BISHOP OF GONDAR AND H.I.M.

Until the university opened in Addis Ababa, Ethiopian students were sent abroad for professional training. Before leaving they were reminded that that they would be serving as ambassadors of their country, and that they should conduct themselves in a manner befitting such. Most lived up to these expectations, not only did they conduct themselves well, they also reflected their tremendous love and attachment for their country. They spoke on behalf of their country and acting on these convictions, they returned home. Prior to the revolution Ethiopians had an easy time traveling. The Dergue would change this, as countries that previously welcomed Ethiopians became wary of a possible refugee problem and subsequent burden on their welfare systems. This legacy continues to this day.

In many respects the Dergue completely reversed the many positive accomplishments of the emperor. Although the Dergue launched a massive literacy campaign for which it received international acclaim and recognition, the overall quality of education in Ethiopia fell drastically. Education beyond the literacy level was strictly controlled and censored. With its denunciation of the monarchical system the Dergue was effectively denouncing the history of the country, invariably tied to the history of its kings and queens. This history was glossed over in schools leaving emerging generations unaware and unappreciative of the tremendous legacy they were inheriting.

The brutality of the Dergue regime was in part responsible for strengthening the desire for independence in Eritrea. By 1991, the independence movement had prevailed and in 1993 Eritrea gained her independence. This marked a significant reversal of one of Emperor Haile Selassie's fundamental achievements, reunion of the ancient coastal province with Ethiopia and acquisition of that treasured access to the sea. Many of the intellectuals and leaders fanning the desires for independence were the children of former unionists who had been ardent supporters of the emperor's efforts to reunite Eritrea with Ethiopia.

In 1991 the EPRDF, a coalition of the various liberation fronts that had emerged during the revolutionary years, succeeded in toppling the Dergue and Ethiopia entered a new period in her history. Soon after EPRDF soldiers had taken control of Addis Ababa the Patriots Association of Ethiopia approached the former rebels informing them that they knew where the emperor was buried and requesting permission to exhume the body so as to provide the emperor, their former patron, with a dignified burial. The search for the grave ensued in the grounds of the *Gibee*, the palace grounds of Emperor Menelik that had served as the headquarters for the Dergue. First to be uncovered was the mass grave of the 'sixty', situated under the open field next to the *Wehni Bet*, or prison at the same spot where they had been gunned down. The emperor's grave proved a little harder to find, until the fragile bones were discovered under the bathroom of Mengistu Haile-Mariam's office.

With the discovery of his grave, a decades old mystery was solved. The final resting-place of the emperor will be with the rest of his family in the grounds of the Holy Trinity Cathedral. There are two marble tombs inside the cathedral where the last imperial couple planned to be buried. Empress Menen's remains have been there since her funeral in 1962 and the tomb next to hers is intended for Emperor Haile Selassie.

According to a senior member of the group that has taken on the responsibility of preparing the funeral and memorial ceremonies for the emperor, in 1995 a group of monks came to Addis Ababa from the countryside with an urgent message. Emperor Haile Selassie had passed away under circumstances that they believed were responsible for the grave ills and misfortune that Ethiopia has experienced over the past twenty-five years. The monks related that during his final days, looking in the direction of the *Entoto Kidane Mihret* (Gospel of Mercy) Church the imprisoned emperor asked, "*Iniam le Ityopia alseranim? Ante Fered*!"– "Have We not also worked for Ethiopia? You be the judge!" With those words the emperor wiped the tears that had welled up in his eyes and flicked them in the direction of the church. Until the people of Ethiopia provide the emperor with a proper burial the monks insisted, the judgment that had come in the form of drought, famine, war, poverty, pestilence, and disease would continue unabated. According to the monks, following the complete mourning period the curse of unrelenting misfortune will be lifted from Ethiopia and a time of prosperity will ensue.

Meanwhile, Crown Prince Asfa Wossen Haile Selassie was crowned Emperor Amha Selassie I of Ethiopia in 1989 by a Crown Council made up of members of a small monarchist movement that endures mostly in exile in Washington DC. In 1998, the would-be emperor passed away and his remains were flown back to Ethiopia where he was laid to rest at the Holy Trinity Cathedral in Addis Ababa.

Emperor Haile Selassie led Ethiopia into the modern era, and that remains his most important legacy. The foundation upon which the future of this historic nation is based was set during his era, and despite the attempts to wipe out this legacy during the Dergue era, it endures. The fundamental changes that will deliver a modern Ethiopian society all have their roots in the accomplishments of Ethiopia's last emperor; everything from the educational system to the basic infrastructure required for developing a modern economy. Although tremendous challenges remain to combat poverty, the means for accomplishing this were set forth by the emperor, his enduring legacy to his people.

1971 HARAR

THE EMPEROR VISITING THE AGRICULTURAL COLLEGE IN HARAR

REFERENCES

Bahru Zewde. *A History of Modern Ethiopia 1855-1974.* Addis Ababa: Addis Ababa University Press, 1991.

Haile Selassie I. *My Life and Ethiopia's Progress* vol. 1. Addis Ababa, 1973. Edited and translated by Edward Ullendorff as the *Autobiography of Emperor Haile Selassie I, 'My Life and Ethiopia's Progress'*, 1892-1937. Oxford, 1976.

Haile Selassie I. *My Life and Ethiopia's Progress*. vol. 2. Addis Ababa, 1974. Edited and annotated by Harold Marcus with Ezekial Gebissa and Tibebe Eshete, Translated by Ezekial Gebissa with Gulumeda Gemede, Tessama Ta'a, Daniel Kendie, Harold Marcus and Angela Raven-Roberts. Michigan University Press, 1994.

Harrison, Paul & Robin Palmer. *News Out Of Africa: Biafra to Band Aid.* London: Hilary Shipman, 1986.

Marcus, Harold G. *Haile Selassie I: The Formative Years, 1892-1936.* London: University of California Press, 1991.

Ministry of Information. *The African Summit Conference.* Addis Ababa: Ministry of Information, 1963.

Ministry of Information. *Biography of an Idea-Story of a Vision Achieved.* Addis Ababa: Ministry of Information, 1973.

Ministry of Information. *Important Utterances of H.I.M. Emperor Haile Selassie I: 1963-1972.* Addis Ababa: Ministry of Information, 1972.

Ministry of Information. *Our Land Ethiopia.* Addis Ababa: Ministry of Information, 1962.

Ministry of Information. *Selected Speeches of Imperial Majesty Haile Selassie I: 1918 to 1967.* Addis Ababa: Ministry of Information, 1967.

Mockler, Anthony. *Haile Selassie's War: The Italian-Ethiopian Campaign, 1935-1941.* New York: Random House, 1984.

Mosley, Leonard. *Haile Selassie: The Conquering Lion.* London: Weidenfeld and Nicolson, 1964.

Pankhurst, Richard. Post World War II Ethiopia: British Military Policy and Action for the Dismantling and Acquisition of Italian Factories and Other Assets. *Journal of Ethiopian Studies* vol. 29, No. 1.

Prouty, Chris. *Empress Taytu and Menelik II: Ethiopia 1883-1910.* Trenton: The Red Sea Press, 1986.

Sandford, Christine. *The Lion of Judah Hath Prevailed.* London: J. M. Dent & Sons Ltd, 1955.

Sergew Hable Selassie. *Ancient and Medieval Ethiopian History to 1270.* Addis Ababa, 1972.

Spencer, John H. *Ethiopia At Bay: A Personal Account of the Haile Selassie Years.* Michigan: Reference Publications, Inc., 1987.

Teferra Haile Selassie. *The Ethiopian Revolution 1974-1991: From A Monarchical Autocracy To A Military Oligarchy.* London and New York: Kegan Paul International, 1997.

Talbot, David Abner. *Haile Selassie I: Silver Jubilee.* The Hague: Stockum and Zoon, 1955.

Thesiger, Wilfred. *The Life of My Choice.* London: Collins, 1987.

PUBLISHED BY

SHAMA BOOKS

P.O.BOX 8153

ADDIS ABABA

ETHIOPIA

Shama@telecom.net.et